muscle

Buicks!

Edited by Thomas E. Bonsall

Osceola, Wisconsin 54020, USA

BOOKMAN PUBLISHING

Baltimore, Maryland

Printed in the U.S.A.
Copyright 1985 in U.S.A. by Bookman Dan!, Inc.

ISBN 0-934780-65-X

First Edition
First Printing

Inquiries may be directed to:
Bookman Dan!, Inc.
P.O. Box 13492
Baltimore, Maryland 21203

Book trade distribution by:
Motorbooks International
P. O. Box 2
Osceola, Wisconsin 54020

A thank you is in order to Mr. William J. Knight,
General Motors Corporation, Public Relations, for
providing the photo of the 1940 Y-Job and the 1953
Wildcat Show Car.

Contents

Buick's Deal of the Century: The First High Performance Machines.

By Robert C. Ackerson

From 1936 through 1942, and again from 1954 through 1958, the Century was the hottest car available from Buick. The fact that Buick offered a car that quickly earned a reputation for a powerful road performance surprised some Buick owners who were not aware that in its formative years Buick was an active competitor in racing events.

The introduction of the Century in 1936, however, did not herald a return to that type of activity. Instead, the Century represented one of the first examples of what was to become the essence of the American supercar: the mating of a powerful engine with a relatively small and lightweight body.

Thus, the first Century, or Series 60 Buick, of 1936 used a 118-inch wheelbase chassis and Buick's new 320.2 cid straight-eight engine. This engine developed 120 hp with a compression ratio of 5.45:1. Compared to its predecessor, it had larger valves, was lighter at 843 lbs and had new Anolite pistons. Buick conservatively credited the Century with a top speed of 95 mph and claimed it accelerated from 10 to 60 mph in 19.6 seconds.

The following year, the Century followed up this successful introduction with attractive new fastback styling in addition to the conventionally styled "Plain Back" models. The Buick engine also came in for some revisions that included the use of aluminum rocker arm shaft brackets and stronger crank and main bearings.

In 1938, Buick made its first use of rear coil springs rather than leaf springs. This development was labeled "Torque Free Springing" and was common to all Buick models. The Buick eight-cylinder engine also had a fancy new term associated with its design, "Turbulator Pistons," which was in reference to its dome-topped pistons. Their use, in addition to some minor refinements, gave the Century a 141 hp rating which, in turn, enabled the Century to reach a top speed of 103 mph.

For 1939, the Buick range received new styling with a grille form and shape that would be mirrored for many years in the front-end appearance of the postwar Buicks. Giving Buick the status of an industry leader were the rear directional lights that were standard on all models. In terms of power, this was not a year of major change for the Century with the most notable new feature being the use of either Stromberg or Carter carburetors in place of the Marvel units used previously.

After expanding its series lineup to include the Super models in 1940, Buick moved to the pinnacle of its (and the Century's) prewar performance heights with the 165 hp, Compound Carburetion engine. This was the most powerful engine available in an American automobile and was equipped with two dual-barrel carburetors (either Carter or Stromberg) and a thinner, 0.15-inch head gasket.

The next year was the final year, not only for Buick production until the war was over, but, it

1936 Buick Model 66S

appeared, for the Century as well. When postwar production began, Buick's plans did not include the Century. Instead, its 1946 lineup called only for Specials, Supers and Roadmasters. In the Brave New World of the Seller's Market there seemed to be no need for a Hot-Rod Buick.

However, that situation didn't have an unlimited life of its own, nor were the automotive tastes of the Americans cast in cement. Once they got their fill of new cars in the years immediately following the end of the war, they began looking for cars that were not just new and shiny, but also exciting to look at, fun to drive and able to accelerate with vigor rather than in a wimpy style. For reasons that really weren't totally founded in fact, Buick was often singled out as the symbol of all that was wrong, in the eyes of foreign sports car fans, with the American car. Its Dynaflow transmission accelerated slowly, its suspension wallowed in the turns and its grille was regarded as a prime example of the American tendency towards bad taste.

This perception, regardless of its accuracy, was totally shattered in 1954 when Buick's new models debuted with styling that was fresh, restrained and extremely contemporary. A new Buick engine had been introduced the previous year, but what it really needed to attract the attention it deserved was a fresh new body style, and that's what it got in 1954.

Moreover, this dynamite combination was given an added shot of adrenalin via the return of the Century series. In its second life, the Century combined the 122-inch chassis of the Special line (which was V-8 powered for the first time) with the 322 cubic inch V-8 that was used for the Super and Roadmaster models. Those Buicks, while approximately 400 lbs heavier than the Century and having a longer, 127-inch wheelbase were not slow cars. For example, "The Autocar" (June 4, 1954) tested a Roadmaster and spoke highly of its "extraordinary performance." The big Buick's time from 0 to 60 mph was just 11.9 seconds, a feat that prompted the testers to note that "on a clear road the red line of the speed indicator moves horizontally across the dial rather like a thermometer which has had a blow lamp applied to its bulb."

"Motor Trend" (February, 1954) was more to the point: "step on the gas and you'll move." Although he managed to get his Century test car from 0 to 60 mph in only 11.8 seconds, Tom McCahill liked it very much, writing in the July, 1954 issue of "Mechanix Illustrated" that, "The 1954 Buick Century is not only the best Buick I've ever driven but one of the nicest handling and feeling cars to come out of Detroit . . . I like it." Joining this chorus of praise for the Century was Griff Borgeson, whose test of a Century Riviera appeared in the April issue of "Motor Life." He found the Century's handling outstanding, claiming that, "the new Buick lends itself to being whipped around tight bends like a small sports car."

The suspension system responsible for this high degree of praise retained the torque tube and four-wheel coil springs of earlier Buicks. What was new and definitely better was a redesigned steering setup

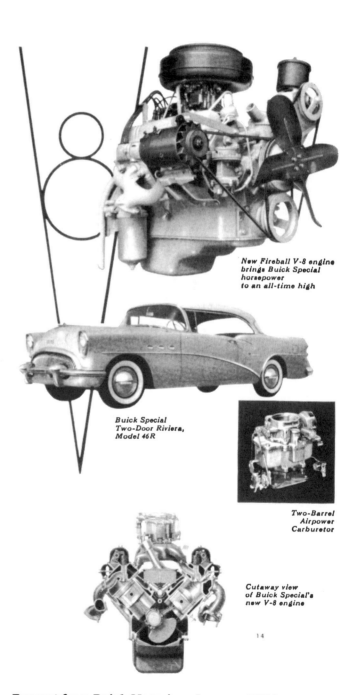

More compact, more powerful, more economical...

BUICK SPECIAL'S NEW V-8 ENGINE

New Fireball V-8 engine brings Buick Special horsepower to an all-time high

Buick Special Two-Door Riviera, Model 46 R

Two-Barrel Airpower Carburetor

Cutaway view of Buick Special's new V-8 engine

Excerpt from Buick Magazine, January, 1954

Buick CENTURY

Back again – Dazzling Performer in Scintill

CENTURY 2-Door 6-Passenger RIVIERA, Model 66R, 122-in. Wheelbase, 200 Horsepower with Dynaflow

TO YOU who recall the Buick CENTURY of prewar years, little more need be said than that this spectacular performer is now back in the line—in modern power and performance and new-day dress.

To you who never knew its prowess—these simple facts will explain the news excitement of the return of the CENTURY:

This is the Buick—reborn in 1954—that has top-of-the-line power in the extra-compact chassis of 122-inches.

Thus, it has the most favorable power-to-weight ratio in Buick history—and the dazzling performance that results from this ratio.

But beyond its 200-horsepower Fireball V8 engine and its highly maneuverable chassis—beyond the beauty of its stunning new body and the rich comfort of its interiors, its visibility, its handling, its ride—the big news of this big-performance automobile is *price*. For the CENTURY returns in 1954 at a price level just a step above Buick's lowest.

ng Dress...

Swing-Away Doors and Tilt-Away Front Seats
insure far more ease in entering and leaving
the spacious interior of the 1954 Century
Riviera. Note the reverse-slant front
pillars that permit an extra-wide sweep
in the panoramic windshield.

1955 Century 2-Door Riviera Model 66R

1955 Century 2-Door Convertible Model 66C

CENTURY 2-Door 6-Passenger Convertible, Model 66C, 122-in. Wheelbase, 236 Horsepower.

1956 Century 2-Door Riviera Model 66R

For the performance-minded...
America's biggest horsepower-per-dollar buy

CENTURY 6-PASSENGER 2-DOOR RIVIERA,
MODEL 66R. 122-IN. WHEELBASE, 255 HORSEPOWER

that consisted of a parallelogram-type linkage, a front suspension with longer wishbones and vertically-mounted, direct-action shock absorbers.

Of course, the Century was best-known for its accelerating ability (Borgeson reported a 0 to 60 mph time of 10.6 seconds) and the source of its reputation was its engine, which developed 200 hp at 4100 rpm and 309 lb-ft of torque at 2400 rpm. Either a Stromberg or Carter four-barrel carburetor was fitted and the Century engine's compression ratio was 8.5:1.

The Century was initially offered in three versions, the Riviera two-door hardtop, a four-door sedan and a four-door Estate Wagon. Later, in May, 1954, a convertible model became available. In terms of appearance, the Century was a clean and uncluttered automobile with three Ventiports, nicely formed twin taillights and a thin side spear. Except for the Century script on the rear fenders, it was easy to mistake a Century for a 143 hp Special, that is, until the light turned green!

Production of the Century totaled 81,982 of which 45,710 were Riviera hardtops. The least popular model was the station wagon whose output was just 1,563.

The popularity of the Century was a major factor in propelling Buick into third place in production ahead of Plymouth in 1954. The next year was even more sensational, both for Buick in general and for the Century in particular. For the model year, a total of 738,814 Buicks were built, of which 159,154 were Centurys.

Along with the rest of the Buick family, the Century received a major restyling for 1955 that, judged by Buick's strong sales, was extremely popular with new-car buyers. Among the most important changes was a reshaped rear fender form that did away with the fender up-kick and replaced the small, bullet-shaped taillights with a much more massive unit incorporating the backup lights. At the front, a stamped grille with a center cross bar was featured that "Motor Life," (March, 1955) described as "definitely more attractive than the toothly former front end." The overall result also pleased "Motor Trend" (March, 1955) which asserted that the "industry could learn from Buick's '55 facelift, which gives new freshness without pointless, too-frequent investments in entirely new dies for all parts."

The Century also was the subject of a good deal of discussion due to its availability as a four-door hardtop in 1955. It shared this distinction among Buicks with the Special series and, during the model run, 55,088 Centurys with this body style were produced.

Nineteen fifty-five was a key year for performance and the Century not only had a new look but also a big boost in horsepower and torque, as well as a new automatic transmission. The net result was a Century that was a major contender for the 0 to 60 mph championship among American cars.

Replacing the Twin-Turbine Dynaflow of 1954 was a Dynaflow with two positions for its stator blades. Under full throttle, the twenty stator blades were angled to get a firmer grip on the transmission fluid, thus providing quicker acceleration. But the real appeal of this Dynaflow was the steeper, 75 degree position the stators assumed when a shift

1956 Century 2-Door Convertible Model 66C

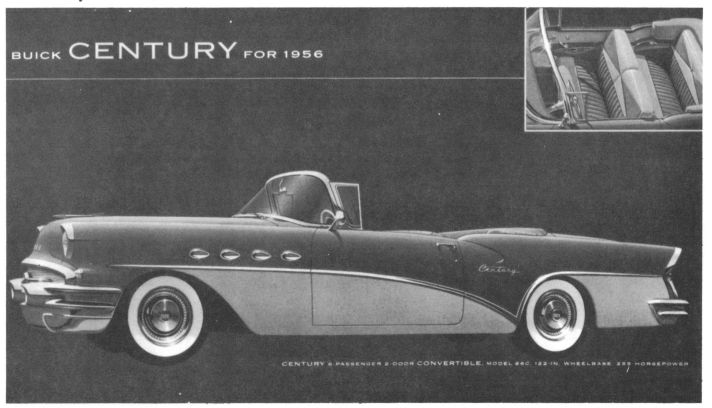

CENTURY 6 PASSENGER 2-DOOR CONVERTIBLE, MODEL 66C, 122-IN. WHEELBASE, 255 HORSEPOWER

NEWNESS FOR THE SAKE OF GREATNESS

You will find that the advances of the 1957 Buick come not in any one place but in totality—not just in look but in engineering throughout.

And the result is a car which transcends newness for itself to bring you to a great new level of American motoring.

Here you see a brand-new kind of styling—sweepingly low in the sports-car tradition—yet wondrously roomier on the inside for six full-sized passengers.

Here you will find a new Variable Pitch Dynaflow—*instant* Dynaflow—so utterly smooth and quickly obedient in its response—so flexible in its power delivery to the rear wheels—it extends the "Drive" range beyond anything you have known before in an automatic transmission.

Pacing this new Dynaflow is a completely new V8 engine—redesigned from the crankshaft up to bring you the mightiest power in all Buick annals and a record high compression to match.

And beneath this Buick beauty is a completely new chassis of ingenious "nested" design to give you a new low center of gravity, better roadability, and a new luxury of ride. Even your handling is done with a new preciseness and ease with Buick's new ball-joint suspension.

So look to your heart's content at the 1957 Buicks on the following pages. Then accept our cordial invitation to drive the newest and most thrilling Buick yet.

Newest Buick Yet

CENTURY 6-Passenger 2-Door RIVIERA, Model 66R, 122-inch Wheelbase, 300 Horsepower

1957 Century 2-Door Riviera Model 66R

1957 Century 2-Door Convertible Model 66C

1957 Century 4-Door Riviera Model 63

CENTURY 6-Passenger 4-Door RIVIERA, Model 63, 122-inch Wheelbase, 300 Horsepower
Similar to the above in room, ride, power—and even more modestly priced—there's the stunning Century 4-Door Sedan, Model 61 (not illustrated).

was made to Low range. Since the Century would run up to 60 mph in Low without difficulty, it was extremely quick from a standing start up to that speed. In its review of the 1955 cars, "Auto Age" (January, 1956) recognized the Buick Century and the Chrysler 300 as America's best performing cars. Although the Chrysler possessed an "unbeatable top speed of nearly 130 mph," reported "Auto Age," it regarded the Buick as "undoubtedly the fastest American production sedan when it comes to initial acceleration, say up to 30, 40, or 50 mph. The Chrysler will just about hold it up to 60 mph."

Other publications supported this conclusion with the results of their road tests of the Century. "Motor Life" (March, 1955) attained a 0 to 60 mph time of 10.9 seconds, but both "Motor Trend" and "Science & Mechanics" reported identical 9.8 seconds times for the same run. Certainly sharing the credit with the new Dynaflow for this accelerating ability was the Century's engine which developed 236 hp at 4600 rpm and 330 lb-ft of torque at 3000 rpm. If a 3-speed manual transmission was installed, the engine's compression ratio dropped to 8.4:1 from 9.0:1.

The Century was, for good reason, extremely popular in 1955 with a model output of 159,154. In total, Buick production reached 718,296 for the model year.

The maximum power of the Century rose to 255 hp at 4400 rpm and 341 lb-ft of torque at 3200 rpm the following year. This placed the Century once again among the fastest accelerating American cars.

1973 Century Gran Sport

Century Turbo Coupe and Century Sport Coupe.

1 Century Sport Coupe.
2 Available bucket seat trim.
3 Available Turbocharged 3.8 litre V-6.
4 Available Century Turbo Coupe.
   Optional tire supplied
   by various manufacturers.

This year, Buick proudly introduces still another new aspect to Century Sport Coupes' form and function, with a new Turbo Coupe Package.

This unique new offering begins with the new Century Sport Coupe and its own attractive list of features. Flat black trim in the grille, around the headlamps and

moldings and a hawk decal. Designers' Sport wheels, wide, steel-belted, radial-ply tires, a Rallye ride-and-handling suspension with fast-ratio power steering when power steering is ordered, sport mirrors and a rear spoiler complete the list. Also standard on the Century Sport Coupe is our Century

Special interior (page 45) full-foam construction be seat trim. Or, if you prefer a somewhat more uptown version, order the availabl elegant Century Custom interior featuring comfort notchback seating, or available 55/45 notchback arrangement (page 46).

Standard Sport Cou

1979 Century Turbo Coupe

is provided by the even- 3.2 litre (196 CID) V-6, is standard on Century ...es and Sedans. Not ...ble in California, where ...litre (231 CID) V-6 with ...atic transmission is ...ble. V-8 engines are also ...ble

...or those who appreciate ...in liveliness, as well

as a distinctive look to their automobile, the Century Turbo Coupe option package features a turbocharged 3.8 litre (231 CID) V-6. It also combines the convenience of things like automatic transmission and power brakes, with the spirit and fun of a Sport steering wheel and sporty dual exhaust system.

Outside, however, is where the difference is really made apparent, with Turbine wheels, a bold Turbo Coupe decal prominently displayed on the trunk, and a turbo hood.

With everything we've told you about them, it may be a little hard by now to think of Century Turbo Coupe or Century Sport Coupe as

practical mid-size cars.

But rest assured, both of them are as adept at being practical, as they are at catching the eye and captivating the spirit.

In a three-way (Buick Century, Packard Clipper and Chrysler Windsor) test conducted by "Auto Age" (August, 1956), the Century was the easy winner in the performance segment with an 8.9-second time for the 0 to 60 mph run. Although other publications reported slightly slower times for this acceleration test, "Motor Life" (May, 1956) duplicated it and Sam Hanks, who tested the Century for "Speed Age" (June, 1956), got his test car down to just 8.10 seconds.

In addition to having more power, the 1956 Century also had its front suspension altered to position the kingpins at a seven-degree angle for both a better ride and handling characteristics, a new Saginaw power steering system and revamped brake linings with grooves to provide both better cooling and less fade.

Styling changes were highlighted by a smoother rear light arrangement, a revamped grille scheme and a functional air scoop nicely blended into the hood ornament's design.

All Buick models had new styling for 1957 that

1985 BUICK CENTURY T TYPE

POWERTRAIN

ENGINE 3.8 Litre MFI V-6

Type	Buick-Bosch multiport fuel injected with electronic mass air flow system 90° V6 arrangement - designed underhood appearance.
Valve Arrangement	Overhead Valve
Bore & Stroke (In.)	3.8x3.4
Displacement (cu.in.)	3.8L (231)
Cylinder Head & Block Material	Cast Iron
Compression Ratio	8.0:1
Net/Installed Horsepower & Engine RPM	125 @ 4400
Net/Installed Torque (lb-ft) & Engine RPM	195 @ 2000
Recommended Fuel	No-lead Reg.
Fuel System Type	Port Fuel Inj.

1983 Century Concept Vehicle

remains to this day controversial, not because it was radical, but because it was seen as too conservative when compared to Chrysler Corporation's "Forward Look." This issue often overshadowed the performance features of the Century which, along with all Buicks, now had a 364 cubic inch V-8.

Buick claimed a 116 mph top speed for the Century, whose power ratings were 300 hp at 4600 rpm and 380 lb-ft of torque at 2400 rpm. This latter figure represented a healthy 50 lb-ft increase from 1956 and enabled the 1957 Century to accelerate from 50 to 80 mph in 3.2 seconds less than the 1956 version.

Although Centurys were losing their hot car image by this time, a review of contemporary road tests suggests that this perception was a bit premature. For example, "Motor Life" (February, 1957) reported a 0 to 60 mph time of 8.7 seconds for its Century test car. This compared favorably to that magazine's test of a Chrysler 300-C which recorded a 7.7-second time for the same run and the 8.2-second mark of a 270 hp Chevrolet. Also often overlooked by the Century's critics was the availability of a special racing kit for the Buick V-8 consisting of 11.1:1 compression ratio pistons, a hotter cam, solid lifters, adjustable rockers and blocked heat risers that raised its horsepower to 330 at 4800 rpm.

The following year, Buick, while retaining the Century series, no longer promoted it as a performance car. Buick was searching for a revised public image to recover its lost sales status of 1957 and plans for 1958 centered around styling that was extremely gaudy and ornate. This quest brought even greater change in 1959 when all Buick series labels were replaced.

Yet, the Century name was only retired temporarily as it turned out. In 1973, it was revived to serve on Buick's line of intermediates and later became the basis of a Gran Sport option. Today's Century is a front-wheel drive automobile that, in its T-Type form, is a legitimate heir to the reputation of Centurys of earlier years. Nearly 50 years separate the first Century from the latest model, and yet they share a common identity as cars that led the crowd rather than followed it.

1985 Century Limited Sedan

The Old Grey Mare Comes to Life: The Exciting Saga of the Gran Sports.

By Robert C. Ackerson·

Although the Gran Sport label was most commonly applied to Buick's mid-sized cars, it made its debut on the 1965 Buick Riviera. When it had been introduced in 1963, the Riviera gained almost immediate acceptance as a high-caliber personal car. With a standard 325 hp engine, the Riviera's performance matched its exciting appearance. In its second year of production, however, the Riviera was available with the first Gran Sport option that, said Buick, was "for those whose love of performance was insatiable." Buick wanted to make this point very clear and, thus, at various times, called the Riviera Gran Sport "a Riviera with muscles on its muscles," the "Executive's Express" and "the latest version of the iron fist in a velvet glove."

Fortunately for the Gran Sport Riviera, it was fully capable of fulfilling these claims and promises with ease. The Gran Sport engine was the standard Riviera 425 cubic inch engine with dual Carter AFB four-barrel carburetors, and a larger diameter dual exhaust system that provided less back pressure.

Enabling the Gran Sport to make the most of this engine's 360 hp at 4400 rpm and 465 lb-ft of torque at 2800 rpm, was a 3.42:1 rear axle with a positive traction differential. Although it wasn't part of the Gran Sport package, Buick offered a heavy-duty suspension system that consisted of firmer springs, shock absorbers and rear track bar bushings. Also included were a heavier front anti-roll bar and faster power steering with a 15:1 ratio instead of the standard Riviera's 17.5:1.

The Gran Sport wasn't a small Buick, of course, with a 117-inch wheelbase and an overall length of 209 inches. Yet, with its strong engine and tight suspension, it could cover a lot of ground quickly an without fuss. In terms of acceleration, the Gran Sport needed, according to "Car and Driver" June, 1965, between 7.0 and 7.7 seconds for the 0 to 60 mph run. For the standing-start quarter-mile drag race, the Gran Sport, which weighed in at over 4,400 lbs, was also very quick, needing just 15.5 seconds to reach the finish line at a speed of 95 mph. "Car and Driver" estimated its maximum speed at 130 mph. "Motor Trend" December, 1964, was only slightly less conservative, noting that the Gran Sport "should be capable of well over 125 mph."

The excellent styling of the basic Riviera body was given only a few subtle touches to distinguish the Gran Sport version from other Rivieras. The most obvious of these were its special full wheel covers and Gran Sport lettering on the rear deck and on the front fenders. Less apparent, at least until the hood was raised, were its polished ribbed valve covers and chromed air cleaner.

The outstanding nature of the Gran Sport Riviera set the stage for the introduction of a Gran Sport version of the Skylark as a mid-1965 model. The Skylark began as an up-market version of the Buick Special in mid-1961. Introduced first as a two-door hardtop with a 185 hp V-8, the Skylark became the third best selling model in Buick's compact car line.

The Skylark's engine was of considerable interest to enthusiasts since it had an aluminum block with cast-iron liners. In addition, other components, such as its pistons, cylinder head, intake manifold and timing chain cover, were also constructed of aluminum. As a result, its installed weight was less than 350 lbs. The following year, the Skylark was offered both as a hardtop and a convertible and its engine was boosted to 190 hp. As appealing as this engine was in many ways, its role in Buick's overall marketing position was limited. The trend was toward V-8s that could be expanded far beyond the bounds of the aluminum V-8. The Skylark's 215 cubic inch V-8 was a fine performer, but to reach its 1963 model year output of 200 hp at 5000 rpm, an 11.0:1 compression ratio had been specified which suggests that further increases in power would have called for some fairly exotic levels of tuning. On the other hand, the more conventional cast-iron block V-8s could turn out prodigious amounts of torque and horsepower with a minimum of fuss.

The result was the replacement of the aluminum V-8 by a 300 cubic inch cast-iron V-8 in the 1964 model year. The previous year, both the Special and thus the Skylark had grown to an overall length of 192.1 inches. This was an increase of nearly four inches from the size of the 1962 models and forecast the blossoming of the 1964 version into an automobile with a wheelbase of 115 inches (up from 112 inches) and a length of 203 inches. At the same time, the Skylark series was expanded to include seven models, one of which, the convertible, was Buick's best-selling softtop.

The Skylark wasn't yet in the ranks of America's top performers, but with the optional 250 hp version of the 300 cid V-8, it wasn't too far off the pace.

Once the Pontiac GTO had successfully broken through the barrier of General Motors' anti-performance policy, the stage was set for the other GM divisions to follow suit. Although General Motors wasn't relenting on its prohibition against actual racing participation, the supercar market was not one that any manufacturer could ignore. Buick made its move in mid-1965, and as expected, it was the Skylark that served as Buick's entry into this sector of the

From Buick Motor Division, General Motors Corporation—a new-size treasure with full-size comfort and a price to pleasantly surprise you.

come challenge the wind

Let your spirits soar in a car that's dynamite from dreamsville ⌁ The Skylark is pure joy ⌁ In the way its flashing Skylark V-8 serves your every command. Yet bows to no one else on the road ⌁ In the way its dapper look thrills you. From bucket-seat* interior to Landau roof lines ⌁ In the way it becomes part of your personality. Part of that secret haven where you store your dreams ⌁ But meet the Skylark soon. It's a limited edition car.

BUICK skylark

*Bucket seats optional at extra cost

Exciting new proof . . . when better automobiles are built / Buick will build them

1964 Skylark

1965 Skylark Gran Sport

1965 Skylark Gran Sport

1965 Skylark GS Tachometer

1965 Skylark GS Floor-Shift 3-Speed

Buick Motor Division

Son of Gun.
The Skylark Gran Sport.
400 cu. in./325 bhp.

Ever prodded a throttle with 445 lb-ft of torque coiled tightly at the end of it?

Do that with one of these and you can start billing yourself as The Human Cannonball.

A floor-shift, all-synchro 3-speed; heavy-duty suspension; low-restriction dual exhausts; oversize, 7.75 x 14 tires; and a high-performance spread of axle ratios—from 2.78 to 3.73:1.

From the makers of the big-bore, 360-bhp Riviera Gran Sport.

The slightly smaller caliber Skylark GS.

Something between a regular Skylark and the Loch Ness Monster.

The Buick Skylark
Gran Sport

Tuned car: the 1966 Buick Wildcat Gran Sport. It's the full-sized family car that purrs quietly. (A wonderful pet to have around.)

market. Initially, the Gran Sport title referred to a performance package that listed for a reasonable $252.86 that was available for three Skylark models: the two-door hardtop, the convertible and the thin-pillar two-door coupe.

All models used the stiffer convertible frame and were powered by the same 401 cubic inch V-8 that was used for Buick's Wildcat, Electra and Riviera models. Since GM policy prohibited the use of any engine larger than 400 cubic inches in its intermediate models, this engine became a 400 cubic-inch V-8 through the magic of the printed word. There were not, however, any falsehoods floating about when it came to the capabilities of this engine. It developed 325 hp at 4400 rpm and 445 lb-ft of torque at 2800 rpm. A single four-barrel Carter AFB carburetor was installed and the engine's compression ratio was 10.25:1. A heavy-duty, cross-flow radiator was also fitted as was a dual exhaust system. The use of this engine in the Skylark chassis required a redesigned left side exhaust manifold. With a weight of 642 lbs, the 401 cid V-8 was 134 lbs heavier than the 300 cid V-8 used in other Skylarks.

Three transmissions were offered for the Gran Sport. The standard unit was an all-synchromesh manual which could be replaced with either a 4-speed manual or a 2-speed Super Turbine 300 automatic modified to handle the added power of the 325 hp V-8.

The suspension of the Gran Sport was highlighted by stiffer front and rear springs with ratings of 420 lb-ft (front) and 155 lb-ft (rear). These contrasted sharply with those used for a base line, six-cylinder Special whose front and rear springs had respective ratings of 305 and 106 lb/ft. In addition, the Gran Sport was equipped with firmer suspension bushings and a larger front stabilizer bar measuring

0.94 inches as compared to the standard unit's 0.75 inches. The Gran Sport was delivered with 7.75-14-inch tires mounted on 6JK rims. Its brakes were unchanged in size from those of other Skylarks, 9.5 x 2.5 inches. However, larger front brake cylinders were used as was a harder lining.

Buick's General Manager, Edward Rollert, described the Gran Sport as "a completely engineered performance car . . . designed to appeal to sports car enthusiasts." In its promotion of the Gran Sport, Buick took a slightly different approach, depicting it as "a howitzer with windshield wipers" and as its owner's "personal-type nuclear deterrent."

This potency was carried about in a very attractive package. The normal Skylark carried a minimum of extraneous trim and the Gran Sport followed this format. Its primary identification elements consisted of red-filled Gran Sport labels on the grille, rear deck and roof pillar. Convertibles had the latter badge placed on their rear fenders. Interior identification was limited to a logo placed on the instrument panel.

In contemporary road tests, the Gran Sport acquitted itself well. For example, "Car Life" May, 1965, reported a time for the 0 to 60 mph run of 7.4 seconds with its test car which had the 2-speed automatic and a 3.08:1 rear axle. Buick offered other rear axle ratios including 2.78, 3.08, 3.36, 3.55 and 3.73. The standard axle for the manual transmission versions was 3.36:1.

To make the Gran Sport an automobile that owners could tailor to meet their individual needs, Buick offered numerous options including chromed steel wheels, a console (for automatic transmission cars) and a tachometer.

Nineteen sixty-six was a banner year for the Gran

The old grey Buick
ain't what she used to be.

There was a time when maybe we didn't build your kind of car.

Times have changed.

There are Buicks coming off our drawing boards these days that would utterly destroy your faith in the established order of sporting machinery.

Tuning is what does it. Not just the engine. The whole car. What we do is take the basic elements of a car—performance, ride, handling, and styling—and tune each to the other so they work together as a balanced unit.

The prime example of our new way of doing things is the 1966 Riviera GS. It's one of our three new Gran-Sports (the other two being the Wildcat GS and the Skylark GS.) Designed as a sports coupe—in the fullest sense of the term—it not only had to look the part but it also had to go, ride, and handle in sporting fashion. And, being a Buick, it had to do all this smoothly, quietly, and with a high degree of creature comfort.

Fitted under its long hood is a 425-cubic inch engine with no less than 340 horsepower and 465 lb-ft. of torque. (Which gets laid down on the road via a

BUICK MOTOR DIVISION

limited-slip differential with a choice of three axle ratios—3.23, 3.42, and 3.58:1.) To give you some small idea of our obsession with how well the engine is put together, we even go so far as to pump hot oil into it under pressure to check for leaks. It all feels rather like you had the world's largest precision watch up front. What it feels like when you open the throttle, however, is something else.

That takes care of moving in a straight line. But since interesting corners are the stuff that serious drivers wouldn't care to live without, we've given the Riviera GS a pretty capable suspension system. It's soft enough to smother any rough stuff you might care to throw under it. Yet, because of the suspension geometry and heavy-duty springs and shocks we've used, it's stiff enough at the same time to give you that sporting handling we were talking about a couple of paragraphs back.

If you're more than normally serious about your driving, something else we've got for the Riviera GS ought to please you: an extra-quick 15:1 power steering gear that you can order. (Now that we mention it, the power steering unit itself is standard; the car doesn't come any other way. As a matter of fact,

the Riviera GS' standard equipment list reads like most other cars' extra-cost options.)

Pikes Peak the wrong way. Now for the final part of a sporting machine: the brakes. The power-assisted system on the Riviera GS is made up of 12-inch finned aluminum drums on the front, 12-inch finned cast iron drums on the rear. We tested them by attacking Pikes Peak from the wrong direction, so to speak. Downhill. In Drive range. Over and over and over again.

The power train. Ride and handling. And styling. All tuned to each other. The tuned car.

Anything else you'd like to know? Instruments? A full complement—needles and numbers and dials and all. Seats? You've a choice. Bench seats and bucket seats are standard. Then there's a special notch-back seat you can order that converts from three-across to semi-buckets.

We've heard it said that the perfect car doesn't exist. Well, then, may we offer you the closest thing?

1966 Buick. The tuned car.

1966 Riviera GS

Sport label at Buick. Both the Riviera and Skylark versions were available, and for the first and only time, a Gran Sport version of the Wildcat was offered. The Wildcat had debuted in 1962 as part of the Invicta series and had become a full series the following year. The Wildcat Gran Sport High Performance Group (to use its official title) listed for $254.71. It included the 340 hp Wildcat 465 V-8 engine (which was outfitted with a chrome-plated air cleaner, cast aluminum rocker arm covers, and dual exhausts), Positive Traction differential, 8.45 x 15 tires (either whitewall or redline) and Gran Sport identification.

The Skylark Gran Sport gained added visual identification via its blacked-out grille, Gran Sport labels in the grille and on the rear deck, simulated twin hood scoops, and a black matte finish for the rear cove panel. No changes were made in the Gran Sport's engine/transmission lineup. As in 1965, the Gran Sport was offered for the $2,956 two-door coupe, $3,019 two-door hardtop and the $3,167 convertible. Although a Gran Sport had the slowest time in the quarter-mile run in a comparison test of six supercars conducted by "Car and Driver" and detailed in its March, 1966 issue, the Buick was far and away the participant nearest to the car that would be purchased for street use. Thus, its speed and time of 95.13 mph and 14.13 seconds was typical of the average Gran Sport.

The second generation Buick Riviera is widely regarded today as one of the best-looking American cars of the modern era, and from that perspective, the Gran Sport version stands out as one of those rare blends of outstanding styling and powerful performance that are the key elements of a classic automobile.

The Riviera and the Riviera Gran Sport had identical engines for 1966. It was the 425 cubic inch V-8 rated at 340 hp. However, a dealer-installed option consisting of twin four-barrel carburetors raised this to 360 hp at 4000 rpm. Maximum torque was 465 lb-ft at 2800 rpm. In this form, and with the optional 3.42:1 rear axle in place of the standard 3.23:1 unit, the Riviera accelerated from 0 to 60 mph in approximately 7.8 seconds. The Gran Sport, which Buick said was for those "who can't get enough of a good thing," was equipped with the high performance suspension and Positraction rear axle. Optional was 15:1 ratio power steering.

All Gran Sport Rivieras had 8.45 x 15 whitewall or redline tires and GS identification just in back of the Riviera script on their front fenders. The same type of identification was also found on its instrument panel.

Buick's use of the GS designation on the 1966 Riviera Gran Sport was applied to its Skylark counterparts the following year. Thus, the Skylark Gran Sport became the GS 400 in 1967. Furthermore, it was joined by a lower priced and less powerful running mate, the GS 340. Whereas the GS 400 was offered as a sport coupe, convertible or thin-pillar two-door coupe, the GS 340 was available only as a two-door hardtop.

Powering the GS 400 was an entirely new 400 cubic inch V-8 that developed 340 hp at 5000 rpm and 440 lb-ft of torque at 3200 rpm. Greeted with an equal amount of enthusiasm from Buick performance fans, who were partial to automatic transmissions, was the availability of Buick's 3-speed, variable-pitch-stator Super Turbine transmission.

As in earlier years, Buick offered many optional

axle ratios for the GS 400. The standard ratio for those equipped with the 3-speed auto was 3.36:1, with 3.55:1 listed as the performance option. Available on special order were 3.90:1 and 4.30:1.

The standard suspension for the GS 400 provided stiffer front and rear springs and a 0.937-inch front stabilizer bar. Although its braking ability was greatly enhanced by finned aluminum drums with iron liners, the GS 400 could be equipped with Moraine front disc brakes.

Visual identification of a GS 400 was easier than ever. Up front was a unique grille with a single center bar incorporating GS letters. These red letters (plus 400 numerals) were also found on the rear deck. Unlike other Skylark models, the GS 400 (and the GS 340) did not have rear fender skirts. Also featured were twin hood scoops, thin side body stripes and 14-inch wheels with F70 x 14 tires of either the whitewall or redline style.

The most popular GS 400 was the two-door hardtop of which 10,659 (that figure includes GS 340 production as well) were built. Its base price was $3,019. The two other models, the thin-pillar coupe and the convertible, were priced respectively at $2,956 and $3,167. They were also very low production models with output levels of 1,014 (coupe) and 2,140 (convertible).

While these prices weren't outrageous, Buick's decision to offer the less expensive GS 340 was a move that anticipated the popular low-priced supercar market that was soon to have many occupants. The GS-340 engine, which to no one's surprise displaced 340 cubic inches, developed 260 hp at 4200 rpm and had a peak torque level of 365 lb-ft. Surprisingly, Buick did not offer the GS 340

with a 4-speed gearbox, or for that matter, a 3-speed automatic. Instead, the only alternative to its standard 3-speed manual transmission was the 2-speed Super Turbine automatic.

The exterior appearance of the GS 340 was distinctive; however, body colors were limited to either white or platinum. These set off broad rally stripes and hood scoops that were given a red finish. In addition, the GS 340's 14-inch wheels were also painted red. The standard tires were 7.75 x 14 rayon cords. Rounding out the GS 340 appearance package were custom moldings along the roof rail and the same type of "vertical lower front ventiports" as found on the GS 400.

The interior of Buick's junior supercar was not elaborate, nor was there much choice offered customers. In fact, they had no choice at all! The only interior available consisted of all-vinyl black bench seats for both the front and rear passengers.

The suspension of the GS 340 included specific front and rear springs and a large diameter front stabilizer bar. An optional "Sport Pac" suspension package included heavy-duty springs and shocks, a heavy-duty rear stabilizer bar and 15:1 ratio steering.

All of General Motors' intermediate models received new styling for 1968 that placed the two-door models on shorter, 112-inch wheelbase chassis. However, it wasn't this more appealing size nor the new GS look that featured a new rendition of Buick's almost legendary side sweep that made the headline news about the GS. That was reserved for its more potent engine lineup.

Replacing the 340 cubic inch engine used in 1967 for the GS 340 was a 350 cubic inch V-8 (its

A phenomenon is arising in this country, and in this time: the new American sporting machines. They're not like the European sports cars. Not at all. America's machines are bred to American driving: they're big and comfortable and roomy and muscular—and at the same time they're amazingly responsive. The epitome of this kind of automobile is Buick's GS-400. A husky, 3,500-pound machine equipped with a 400-cubic-inch, 340-horsepower V-8 and a sporting feel. It's all the car anyone could want.

the GS-340

1967 GS-340

1967 GS-400

And now the GS-400 has a running mate: the new Buick GS-340. This one is for people who look for a large measure of sporting flavor at a low price. (Until now, it's been a long, hopeless search.)
In these pages, you'll learn a lot about the mechanics of these two machines. You can read all the specifications and look at all the pictures. But they won't come to life until you put them into action.
And until you do that, you really won't know how pale your own driving has been.

the GS-400

1967 GS-400 Convertible

1968 Skylark GS

1968 GS-350

30, The Exciting Saga of the Gran Sports

1968 GS California

1969 GS-400

use required a name switch to GS 350), that provided 280 hp at 4600 rpm and 375 lb-ft of torque at 3200 rpm. A 3-speed manual was the standard transmission, but a 4-speed gearbox was optional as was the 2-speed automatic. Both of the manual transmissions were regarded as heavy-duty models and could be linked to an extra-cost Hurst linkage. The 350 engine was fitted with heads and intake and exhaust manifolds that were similar to those used on the 430 cubic inch V-8. As in 1967, the junior Gran Sport was not available with the 3-speed Turbo Hydra-Matic transmission, however, both the optional heavy-duty 3- and 4-speed transmissions could be equipped with Hurst linkage.

The GS 400 engine was essentially unchanged for 1968. The only major revision was the addition of a "controlled emission system." This was an important year for Gran Sport performance since the basic GS 400 engine could be upgraded significantly via a dealer-installed option known as the "Stage I Special Package." This included a cam with greater lift and duration, 11.0:1 compression ratio, forged pistons with solid skirts, stronger valve springs and revised spark advance curve, and carburetor calibration. Buick officially rated this engine at 345 hp at 4800 rpm and 440 lb-ft of torque at 3200 rpm, however, most engine authorities considered the Stage I V-8 to have a horsepower output closer to 400. If this wasn't enough to please the Super-Buick enthusiast, there was also a Stage II engine with an even greater output.

Although the thin-pillar coupe was dropped from the GS line for 1968, this was the best sales year for Buick's supercar to date. A total of 21,514 were built of which 2,514 were convertibles. Output of the GS 350, which was included in this figure, was 8,317.

As a mid-year sales stimulant, Buick offered the California GS, which it described as "the distinctive personal car for Americana on the go." In essence, this was the GS 350 with special trim. The 2-speed automatic was standard as was a vinyl top, chrome exterior trim and special chrome plated "super sport" wheels. GS California trim was placed on the grille, roof sail panels and the rear fenders.

The late sixties and early seventies are generally regarded as the years of fulfillment for the supercar in America and, for the GS Buick, it was a time of both maturity and performance excellence.

The 1969 versions on the 112-inch wheelbase were still offered in GS 400, GS 350 or California GS form. Styling changes were not extensive since this was just the second year for their basic body shell. Typical of the changes made were a new grille with a thick center bar, vertical rather than horizontal front fender trim plates, the removal of the front vent windows, and a considerably more prominent hood scoop arrangement. This latter feature wasn't merely a cosmetic change since it was part of Buick's new "Cool Air" induction system. The new GS hood had twin scoops that were linked to a special air cleaner with twin snorkels. Although Buick left the

1970 GS Stage I

Following pages, 1970 GSX Brochure

MEET A BRAND-NEW BRAND OF BUICK...GSX

HOOD TACH! Be able to tell engine RPM's at a glance with the hood-mounted tachometer. It lets the driver know what his powerplant is doing for him and when it's the proper time to shift. Illuminating level can be varied along with other instrument lighting by adjusting the headlamp rheostat.

BILLBOARDS! Traction is improved with fat, wide-tread G60-15 tires mounted on big 15-inch chrome-plated wheels that are a full 7 inches wide. Large white billboard letters provide the sporty, appearance.

SPOILERS! Stylish, molded fiberglass rear deck spoiler acts with the front spoiler which is tucked under the bumper of every GSX. They help keep the front and rear end down for improved traction and handling.

SPORTS MIRRORS! Two outside rear-view mirrors let the driver know what is going on behind. Streamlined protective covers are painted to match the car. The driver's side Sports Mirror is easily adjustable by remote control from inside the car.

GSX shown in Saturn Yellow. Also available in Apollo White.

-SPEED BOX!
his close-ratio 4-
eed manual trans-
ission provides
sponsive perfor-
ance. Shifting is
sy because it
fully synchro-
zed in all forward
ars. The smooth-
erating Hurst linkage is stan-
rd. A floor-mounted consol-
te adds sports car flavor.
ree-speed Turbo Hydra-matic
0 automatic transmission with
erating console is available.

BUCKETS! Soft, supple, all-
vinyl, custom-padded bucket
seats are standard on the GSX.
Black Madrid- and Laredo-grain
vinyl are tastefully combined to
create a stylish interior. Special
GSX ornamentation is included.

455-4! Deep-breathing 455-
cubic-inch powerplant provides
350 horsepower and a new
brand of Buick performance. In
addition, there is the Stage 1
option available which develops
360 horsepower and a maximum
torque of 510 pounds feet.

MORE! MORE! MORE!
Buick puts even more standard
equipment into the GSX. A
rallye clock and engine operat-
ing gauges. A 15-inch-diameter
vinyl-covered rallye steering
wheel. Special, quick-ratio variable ratio power steering is
available. A 3.42 ratio positive
traction rear axle. Power front
disc brakes. Heavy duty cooling. Buick GSX performance car
handling is the result of several more features like large
diameter front and rear stabilizer bars, heavy duty front and
rear shock absorbers, firm ride
control arms and control arm
bushings. And special GSX
ornamentation inside and out.
GSX...Something to Believe In!

BUICK GSX SPECIFICATIONS

ENGINE	Standard	Available Stage 1 Option
Type	90° V-8	90° V-8
Valve Arrangement . .	In-head	In-head
Bore and Stroke (inches)	4.3125x3.90	4.3125x3.90
Displacement (cu. in.)	455	455
Compression Ratio	10.0:1	10.5:1
Horsepower at Engine RPM . . .	350 @ 4600	360 @ 4600
Torque (lbs.-ft. at Engine RPM) . . .	510 @ 2800	510 @ 2800
Valves:		
Intake (dia. in.) .	2.005-1.995	2.005-1.995
Exhaust (dia. in.)	1.630-1.620	1.630-1.620
Camshaft	Intake Exhaust	Intake Exhaust
Lift (in.)	.3891 .4602	.490 .490
Duration (degrees) . . .	290 322	316 340
Overlap (degrees) . . .	67	90
Tappets	Hydraulic	Hydraulic
Carburetion:		
Make	Roch. Quadra-jet	Roch. Quadra-jet
Type	4-barrel	4-barrel
Primary Bores (in.) . . .	1.375 dia.	1.375 dia.
Secondary Bores (in.) . . .	2.250 dia.	2.250 dia.
Exhaust	Dual-Low Restriction	Dual-Low Restriction

DIFFERENTIAL Type: Positive Traction —Limited Slip. Ring Gear Diameter (inches): 8.500. Final Drive Gear Ratios: GSX, 3.42, GSX Stage 1, 3.64, 3.42 with A/C.

CLUTCH Type: Dry. Total Spring Load (pounds): 2450-2750. Outside/Inside Diameter (inches): 11.0/6.5. Total Effective Area (square inches): 123.7. Lining Thickness (inches): .140.

STEERING	MANUAL	AVAILABLE POWER
Gear Ratio	24:1	14.6:1 to 11.0:1
Overall Ratio	28.6:1	17.0:1 to 13.6:1
Turning Circle (curb-to-curb) (feet) .	39.9	39.9
Wheel Turns (lock-to-lock)	5.6	3.4
Wheel Diameter (inches)	15	15

70-BA-71   Litho in U.S.A.

TRANSMISSIONS Type: 4-speed manual—synchronized in all forward speeds. Gear Ratios: First 2.20, Second 1.64, Third 1.28, Fourth 1.00, Reverse 2.27. Type: Available 3-speed Turbo Hydra-matic automatic with 3-element torque converter. Maximum Ratio at Stall: 2.05. Gear Ratios (each times converter ratio): First 2.48, Second 1.48, Third 1.00, Reverse 2.08.

BRAKES Front: 11.0-inch vented disc, power assisted. Rear: 9.5-inch diameter finned composite cast iron drum, power assisted. Total Swept Area (sq. in.): 323.0. Total Effective Area (sq. in.): 104.2.

WHEELS & TIRES Wheel Size (inches): 15 x 7.00. Tire Size and Description: G60-15 White billboard lettered fiberglass belted.

SUSPENSION Type: Front—Independent with coil springs and ball joint; Rear—One-piece rear housing with coil springs and upper and lower control arms. Spring Rates: Front (pounds per inch)—450; Rear (pounds per inch)—144. Shock Absorbers: Direct-acting, 1-inch-diameter pistons. Stabilizer: Front—1.00 inch diameter—link type; Rear—.875 inch diameter —linkless.

DIMENSIONS

Wheelbase (inches) 112.0		Minimum Ground	
Front Tread (inches) 60.12		Clearance (inches) 6.42	
Rear Tread (inches) 59.0		Trunk Capacity (cubic feet) . .12.6	
Overall Height (inches) 53.0		Fuel Tank Capacity	
Overall Length (inches) 202.0		(approx. gallons) 20	
Overall Width (inches) 77.3		Curb Weight (pounds) 3874	

Add 45.7 pounds for automatic transmission option.   Add 2.4 pounds for Stage 1 option.

1970 GSX

GS engine ratings unchanged from 1968, it also claimed that this system increased maximum horsepower by eight percent and provided a six-and-one-half percent boost in peak torque. Still available were the Stage I and II options.

For the 1970 model year, General Motors relaxed its edict prohibiting the use of engines larger than 400 cubic inches. The result was a Gran Sport with a 455 cubic inch V-8. The GS 455 was produced as a convertible or two-door hardtop. In either form, it was an impressive supercar with ratings of 350 hp at 4600 rpm and a whopping 510 lb-ft of torque at 2800 rpm. The GS 455's running mate was known simply as the GS for 1970 which really was a bit of a pity since its 350 cid V-8 now turned out a healthy 310 hp at 4800 rpm and 410 lb-ft of torque at 3200 rpm. Somehow, a reasonably priced and attractive automobile as the GS deserved a title that gave just a little more of a hint about its ability.

But no one could suggest that Buick was shy about promoting its very limited production (only

678 were built) mid-year offering, the GSX. This was technically a $1,196 option for the GS 455 consisting of a hood-mounted tachometer with a variable lighting control, G60 x 15 tires on seven-inch wide, chrome-plated wheels, molded plastic front and rear spoilers, twin exterior mirrors, a 4-speed manual transmission, front disc brakes, heavy-duty suspension and black vinyl bucket seats. In addition, the GSX had special grille and instrumentation ID plates. The only two exterior colors available were Saturn Yellow and Apollo White.

The GSX standard engine was the GS 455 V-8, but it was also available (as was the GS 455) with the 360 hp Stage I version.

Buick did not offer the GSX the following year which saw the Gran Sport's base engine become a mild 260 hp, 350 cid V-8. Two versions of the 455 cid V-8 were optional, rated at 315 and 345 hp. The age of restrictive emission regulations had arrived and were taking their toll upon the supercars.

After a production run of 20,096 Gran Sports in

1970 Riviera GS

1971 Riviera GS

1974 Century Gran Sport

1970, output dropped to 9,170 for the 1971 model run. This poor sales performance pointed the way towards the Gran Sport's demise, at least on the Skylark platform the next year. These versions were also produced in small numbers, with a total production run of just 8,575 cars. Their base engine had a net horsepower rating of 195, while the optional 455 cid had 225 hp. The Stage I version was rated at a respectable 275 hp.

In both 1973 and 1974, Buick offered a Gran Sport edition of the Century which had returned as a Buick series in 1973. The Century was a very handsome Buick with a wheelbase of 112 inches and an overall length of 210 inches. The major features of the Gran Sport package in both 1973 and 1974 included a Rallye ride and handling package which encompassed front and rear stabilizer bars, a blacked-out grille and headlamp doors, rear deck accent stripe, special rear lights with thin vertical dividers, an instrument gauge cluster, wheel well molding, and Gran Sport identification. The price of this package on a 1973 Century was $108. If the 225 hp, 455 cid engine was desired, it came as part of the GS 455 option which included dual exhausts and power front disc brakes. Its price was $292. Buick took this engine a bit farther up the performance ladder via a dual snorkle air cleaner

which was priced at $338. Finally, the top-rated (and priced) Gran Sport had the Stage I engine with (in 1974) 255 hp at 4400 rpm, and 370 lb-ft at 2800 rpm. Included in this package was a limited slip rear axle. All Gran Sports with the Stage I option were required to be equipped with Turbo-Hydramatic 400 transmission.

The last Buicks to be available in Gran Sport form were the 1975 Rivieras. After the 1966 model year, Buick had made the Gran Sport option for the Riviera a handling and appearance package that was not joined to a particular engine. For example, the 1974 version consisted of a rear stabilizer bar, J78 whitewall steel-belted tires, additional sound insulation and special body trim. It could also be ordered with the Stage I engine which, in Riviera form, had 245 hp and 360 lb-ft of torque.

As it had in pre-war years, and in the early fifties with the Century, Buick never intended the Gran Sport to be just another quick car. Instead, it was first and foremost a Buick and that made it a supercar with both class and power. Although they never were the best-selling cars of their type, the Gran Sports were always highly regarded by enthusiasts, many of whom viewed them as examples of Buick's ability to build a better supercar.

1975 Riviera-GS was a handling
    package at this time with specific
    GS ornamentation

More Power to You: The Story of the Buick V-8.

By Robert C. Ackerson

Although Buick trailed Oldsmobile and Cadillac, as well as Chrysler, DeSoto and Studebaker in the introduction of postwar V-8s, it has been involved in V-8 engine research and development for many years. In 1931, Buick considered production of a "twin-six" and, starting in 1944, an ongoing project involving V-8 engines was started. To carry on this work, a special department was established which built over 100 experimental models and evaluated 10 different types of engines.

As Buick amassed a large data bank about the various cylinder 'V' angles and combustion chamber shapes, an early favorite emerged in the form of a 35 degree 'V' engine. This engine had one serious, and as events fell into place, fatal flaw: its carburetor height could not be reduced enough to allow its use in the cars that were being designed by General Motors for the postwar market.

This issue was of paramount importance in an age when styling would be a major selling point. In their SAE paper dealing with the development of the first Buick V-8, Verner P. Mathews and Joseph D. Turley noted, "We do not believe that the V engine has any inherent advantages over the in-line engine in regard to power or economy." There were, however, four major reasons for Buick's conversion to V-8 power cited by Mathews and Turley and the first concerned styling. "The proportions of the 'V' engine," they explained, "are more suitable for installation in cars with the newer styling and particularly in cars with the styling which General Motors believes will be standard several years from now." To further support their view, Mathews and Turley noted that the XP-300 and LeSabre, (which they regarded as the "cars of the future"), had 90-degree V-8s because that "was the only design which we could fit within the allotted space under the hood."

There were, however, many good, solid engineering advantages to the V-8 that made it a desirable engine. For example, it was more compact, inherently lighter than an equivalent in-line engine and more rigid and capable of withstanding the combustion pressures resulting from the use of high-compression ratios. Certainly not the least significant factor behind Buick's decision to go V-8 was that it was time for a change! After all, the tooling for the Roadmaster straight-eight dated back to 1936.

Work on the Buick Fireball V-8 began in 1950, and if the Korean War had not taken place, the chances were excellent that it would have been in production earlier than 1953. When first introduced

in 1953, the Buick's 4.0-inch bore and 3.2-inch stroke gave it a very low 0.8 stroke-bore ratio. Its displacement of 322 cubic inches was only slightly greater than the old straight-eight's 320 cubic inches. Yet its weight, at 624 lbs, was 170 lbs less than the straight-eight's. Some specific examples of weight reduction included a five-bearing crankshaft which, at 56 lbs, weighed less than half than the crank used in the 1952 Roadmaster engine. Furthermore, the V-8's block and crankcase was, at 176.5 lbs, approximately 72 lbs lighter than the 1952 version.

While the Buick V-8's ability to rev to 5500 rpm before the hydraulic lifters began to pump up was welcomed, there was considerably less enthusiasm for its small-sized valves. These were placed vertically to make the engine more compact, lighter, and easy to manufacture. Buick anticipated criticism for the small 1.50-inch exhaust valves (the intakes measured 1.875 inches) and as the men on the spot, Mathews and Turley came out swinging, citing the 1909 Buick Bug as an example of Buick's recognition of the "value of an inlet valve of much larger size than the exhaust valve." Although these words often fell on unbelieving ears, Mathews and Turley maintained that Buick's use of a relatively small exhaust valve "made a more compact combustion chamber, improved valve cooling, and reduced cost without entailing any loss in power."

Far less controversial was the design of the V-8's combustion chamber which was fully machined, enabled the spark plug to be centrally located and

1946 Buick Fireball Dynaflash Eight Sectional View

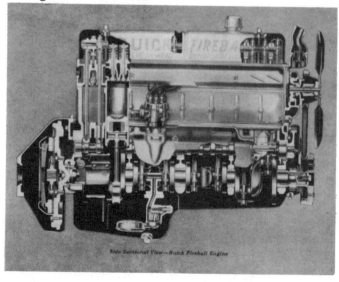

Side Sectional View—Buick Fireball Engine

1953 XP-300 Experimental

utilized an inverted V form. In addition to its high 8.5:1 compression ratio, the combustion chamber provided excellent gas turbulence as well as very short flame travel.

Buick subjected its new engine to over 10,000 hours of dynamometer testing as well as 1,000,000-plus miles of road operation at the General Motors Proving Ground. Mathews and Turley candidly admitted that the "usual quota of corrections have been made as faults developed." They were also justifiably proud to report that the second experimental engine assembled in the fall of 1950 "ran on full throttle high speed endurance at 4200-4500 rpm several hours longer than any of the notably rugged straight-eight Roadmaster engines have ever run in the same standard test."

A harbinger of the future came in the form of

The XP-300

Tomorrow's Evidence that When Better Automobiles Are Built BUICK Will Build Them

Buick's power claims for its new V-8. Mathews and Turley noted that "because of the current contest in advertised horsepower, we approach the subject of engine output with some misgivings. The problem of whether to try to out-exaggerate the field or to quote actual figures, which may not seem sufficiently high to some, is a difficult choice." But the cold, hard facts placed the Buick V-8 in a highly favorable position. Comparative tests of four competitive V-8s by Buick and the results of additional tests by other General Motors divisions, General Motors Research and the General Motors Technical Center indicated that no American engine available in 1952 exceeded the Buick engine's horsepower ratings under the same testing conditions.

At the outset of its production, Buick claimed the new V-8 would be at least as durable as the old straight-eight, would deliver approximately eight percent fuel economy and be seven percent less

THE PERFECT COMBINATION

The Offenhauser "Eldorado" Type Dual Quad Manifold

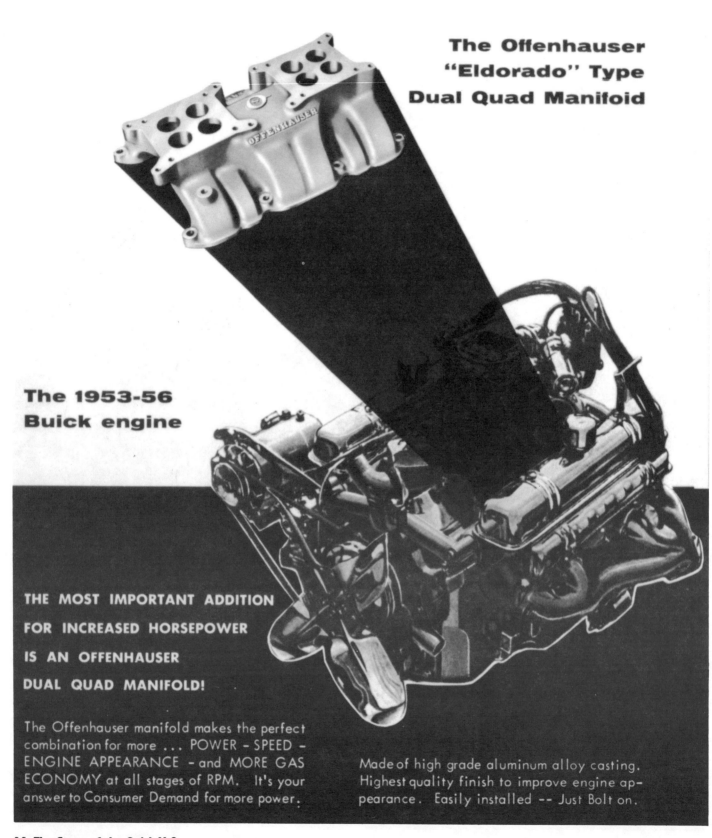

The 1953-56 Buick engine

THE MOST IMPORTANT ADDITION
FOR INCREASED HORSEPOWER
IS AN OFFENHAUSER
DUAL QUAD MANIFOLD!

The Offenhauser manifold makes the perfect combination for more ... POWER - SPEED - ENGINE APPEARANCE - and MORE GAS ECONOMY at all stages of RPM. It's your answer to Consumer Demand for more power.

Made of high grade aluminum alloy casting. Highest quality finish to improve engine appearance. Easily installed -- Just Bolt on.

POWER

POWER

Offenhauser EQUIPMENT CORP.
5156 ALHAMBRA AVE., LOS ANGELES 32, CALIF

1954 Variable Pitch Dynaflow, 236 hp

expensive to produce. Finally, Buick claimed its V-8 was "the lightest and most compact engine for its power output now in quantity production in America."

During its production run, which lasted until the 1967 model year, the Buick V-8 was refined, enlarged and increased in its torque and horsepower ratings. In 1954, a smaller, 264 cubic inch version was introduced for the Special series which had used a straight-eight in 1953. That year, Buick also used "Power-Head" pistons with a lower and flatter dome and a longer skirt length. These provided a combustion chamber with a greater volume-to-air ratio.

Two years later, in 1956, all series used the 322 cubic inch version. The previous year the V-8's compression ratio was raised from 8.5:1 to 9.0:1 and larger, 1.375-inch exhaust valves were fitted. The first displacement boost took place in 1957 when a larger 4.125-inch bore and 3.40-inch stroke were used to yield 364 cubic inches. Two years later, a 401 cubic inch version with a 4.1875-inch bore

Much of the thrill is in the engine

THERE'S NEW BUICK POWER...
AND LOTS MORE OF IT

New record-high compression —up to 9 to 1 ratio

New "full-skirt" slotted pistons for minimum friction

Buick steps up pickup still more with a <u>new</u> Variable Pitch Dynaflow

Buick engineers really had to go some to top the performance of last year's Variable Pitch Dynaflow.

For this new kind of automatic transmission adapted the principle of aviation's variable pitch propeller to land travel—and it took the country by storm.

One pitch of the propeller-like blades spinning in Dynaflow oil gave dazzling take-off and passing power when needed. The other pitch gave new gas economy at cruising speed.

Now, to this spectacular transmission, Buick engineers have added still greater pickup and gas savings in 1956.

Source of this new thrill in Dynaflow is a second stator—a second set of propeller-like blades—which delivers a record power thrust to the rear wheels.

Now you nudge the pedal—and instantly you move into motion with a silken swiftness more solid than flooring the pedal would do before.

Now you get better gas mileage because you get better pickup without opening the throttle wide.

But when you do need to open the throttle to level a steep hill or to pass quickly and safely, you switch the pitch and off you go with power that sinks you in your seat.

So this new double-action take-off of Variable Pitch Dynaflow —especially as it's teamed to the 1956 Buick's increased power —is something that thrills you the first time you try it and from then on. It is the only Dynaflow Buick builds and is standard on ROADMASTER, SUPER and CENTURY Series, optional at extra cost on the SPECIAL Series.

Buick V8 power rises to great new peaks

...220 IN THE SPECIAL
...255 IN THE ROADMASTER, SUPER AND CENTURY

Heart of the great Buick performance which wings you along your way with such sparkle and dash in 1956 is a 322-cubic-inch V8 engine, Buick engineered and Buick built. The complete adaptability of this compact power plant's basic design to take on new advances, as Buick engineers perfect them, may be seen more clearly this year than ever before. For here, Buick engineers have brought new life and lift with a host of improvements. Among the more important of these you'll find—

All-Time-High Compression Ratios—9.5 to 1 in the 255-horsepower ROADMASTER, SUPER and CENTURY engines with 4-Barrel Airpower Carburetors.

8.9 to 1 in the 220-horsepower SPECIAL engine with 2-Barrel Carburetor.

New Combustion Chamber Design — Increases flow of fuel-air mixture *into* cylinder and exhaust gas *out of* cylinder — increases power output.

New Double "Y" Exhaust Manifolds — Increase power output considerably by relieving each cylinder of its exhaust gases through separated manifold branches. New dual-exhaust system, standard on ROADMASTER and optional on other Series.

More Rugged High-Alloy Forged Steel Crank-shaft and Connecting Rods

PLUS—Smoother engine warm-up with Built-in Carburetor De-Icer ★ Powerful 12-Volt Electrical System ★ Buick-originated Vertical Valves ★ Exclusive leakproof, extra-quiet Ball Joint Exhaust System

Should only strong, steely-nerved men be permitted to drive this '64 Wildcat?

Buick Motor Division

The only reason we raise this question is because we're talking about the toughest, meanest, most impatient Wildcat Buick's ever bred. The one with the optional-at-slight-extra-cost Super Wildcat engine. It's Buick's top output V-8 (if you know your engines, nuff said), and here's some inside dope on what makes it so "super." Horsepower—360 at 4400 rpm; displacement—425 cu. in.; compression—10.25:1; torque—465 ft.-lbs. at 2800 rpm; plus a couple of 4-bbl. downdraft carbs. To keep pace with this all fired up V-8, we suggest either the new, instant response Super Turbine 400 automatic or our 4-on-the-floor synchro. Now, do you think you're the "Super Wildcat" type? Find out—at your Buick dealer's. Drive the Wildcat—

above all, it's a Buick

1967 430-4 V-8

and 3.65-inch stroke was available. The largest model of the original Buick V-8 arrived in 1963 with a bore of 4.188 inches and an unchanged stroke of 3.64 inches which provided a displacement of 425 cubic inches. This engine reached its peak power output in 1966 with 360 hp and 465 lb-ft torque ratings.

This engine had also reached the outer limits of its growth potential, and in an age of explosive performance, it was time for a new Buick V-8 to arrive on the scene. In 1964, Buick had introduced a 300 cubic inch V-8 for its Special series. Two years later, this V-8's stroke was increased from 3.40 inches to 3.85, which expanded its displacement to 340 cubic inches. This engine wasn't completely new since it was heavily influenced by both the aluminum V-8 and the Buick V-6.

By contrast, the two V-8s Buick began to use for its 1967 models had virtually all-new tooling and represented an investment of over $50 million. The smaller version, with 400 cubic inches, was rated at 340 hp at 5000 rpm and was used for the Gran Sport. The larger engine, with 430 cubic inches and 360 hp at 5000 rpm powered the Wildcat, Electra and Riviera models. Both versions had a stroke of 3.9 inches and respective bores of 4.04 and 4.1875 inches.

Cliff Studaker, Buick's chief engine engineer, explained the motive behind the development of these engines in very simple terms: "We at Buick felt we needed a new big V-8. The old design dated basically from 1953 and we had developed it about as far as we could." Among its major design features were valves inclined at 15 degrees, a semi-wedge combustion chamber and a cast nodular crankshaft in place of the older engine's forged unit. The intake and exhaust valves measured 2.0 and 1.625 inches, respectively, which was an increase of 0.125 inches over those of the 1966 V-8. Also reflecting solid improvement was the new V-8's 11 percent larger intake port cross section areas and its exhaust ports whose area was 80 percent greater. These V-8 engines had a relatively short production run. The 400 cubic inch version was not offered after the 1969 model year and the larger version, which was bored out to provide 455 cubic inches in 1970, was dropped after the 1976 models. The last of the true Buick V-8s displaced 350 cubic inches and was derived from the 340 cubic inch small block V-8.

1967 Riviera GS, Wildcat, Electra 225

WHAT ARE THE UNION 76 PERFORMANCE TRIALS?

The Union 76 Performance Trials run at Daytona Beach, Florida, are impartially run tests of cars manufactured in the United States. The trials are sponsored by the Union Oil Company and consist of three competitive events . . . acceleration, economy and braking. All the cars are purchased by the Union Oil Company from regular retail dealers. These cars are built, and equipped the same as a car you would buy.

The performance trials were completely staffed and supervised by National Association for Stock Car Racing (NASCAR) personnel.

The cars are grouped into nine classes. Each car competes within its assigned class in three events . . . acceleration, economy and braking. Points are compiled and awards are made to the car manufacturer whose car turns in the best overall performance in each class.

The economy test demonstrates fuel economy of cars under average city and freeway driving conditions. The acceleration test measures the car's capability of passing on a two-lane road or entering an expressway. Braking test results show the ability of a vehicle to make a high-speed emergency stop immediately following severe brake usage such as on an expressway or during descent of a mountain.

To assure equal testing, each car is driven for a break-in period of 1400 to 1500 miles. All cars in a given class are tested on the same day in all three events so each car in that class is tested under similar competitive conditions. This year the performance trials were run from January 18 through 22 at the NASCAR testing facilities at Daytona Beach, Florida.

BUICK VALUE PROVED AT UNION 76 PERFORMANCE TRIALS!

GS-455 over-all Class VII winner!

To be an over-all class winner, GS-455 accumulated more total points than its competition. Points were awarded on the results of economy, acceleration and braking tests. Buick GS-455 placed first in economy, third in braking, fourth in acceleration and was the overall winner of Class VII by out-performing all five competitive cars in the class.

These cars had standard wheels and tires, radio, automatic transmission, power steering, power brakes and any additional options that happened to be on the cars when they were selected by NASCAR for the Union Oil Company. Axle ratios and engines were specified by NASCAR.

Class II acceleration won by Wildcat!

A 1970 Buick Wildcat Custom demonstrated its ability as a performer by winning the acceleration portion of Class II competition in the Trials. It was second in economy and braking and finished second over-all in this class. Class II was made up of Deluxe 8-cylinder cars.

For agility on the road . . . wouldn't you really rather have a Buick?

Class I swept by Riviera and Electra 225!

For the second year in a row, first place in Super Deluxe Class competition was won by a Buick Riviera. Second place was won by a Buick Electra 225.

In the three individual tests, Riviera placed first in economy, first in acceleration and second in braking. Electra 225 placed first in braking, second in economy and third in acceleration.

Each car in this class was equipped with power steering, power brakes, automatic transmission, air conditioning, radio and various optional equipment. Standard engines, wheels, tires and rear-axle ratios were specified by NASCAR.

Buick Riviera and Electra 225 out-performed all four competitive cars in the class to make a clean sweep of Class I.

With results like this . . . wouldn't you really rather have a Buick?

1974 Buick
OPTIONS AVAILABILITY

1974 Buick available equipment	Apollo	Century 350/Century Luxus	Gran Sport	Regal	Century 350/Century Luxus Station Wagons	LeSabre/LeSabre Luxus	Estate Wagon	Electra 225/Electra Custom/Electra Limited	Riviera
LeSabre Luxus ride and performance package						Avail.			
Riviera GS handling package									Avail.
Power assist on front disc brakes	Avail.	Avail.	Avail.	Avail.	Std.	Std.	Std.	Std.	Std.
Variable-ratio power steering	Avail.	Std.	Std.	Std.	Std.	Std.	Std.	Std.	Std.
Quick-ratio power steering			Avail.						
High-energy ignition system	Avail.	Avail.	Avail.	Avail.	Avail.	Avail.	Avail.	Avail.	Avail.
Dual exhaust		Avail.	Avail.	Avail.	Avail.	Avail.	Avail.	Avail.	Std.
Positive traction differential	Avail.	Avail.	Avail.	Avail.	Avail.	Avail.	Avail.	Avail.	Avail.
Firm ride and handling package	Avail.	Avail.		Avail.	Avail.	Avail.	Avail.	Avail.	Avail.
Trailer towing suspension package	Avail.	Avail.		Avail.	Avail.	Avail.	Avail.	Avail.	Avail.
Automatic level control		Avail.	Avail.	Avail.	Avail.	Avail.	Avail.	Avail.	Avail.
Superlift shock absorbers		Avail.	Avail.	Avail.	Avail.	Avail.	Avail.	Avail.	Avail.
Heavy-duty wheels		Avail.		Avail.		Avail.	Std.	Avail.	Avail.
Heavy-duty engine and transmission cooling	Avail.	Avail.	Avail.	Avail.	Avail.	Avail.	Avail.	Avail.	Avail.
MaxTrac						Avail.	Avail.	Avail.	Avail.
Oversize whitewall tires		Avail.	Avail.	Avail.	Std.	Avail.	Avail.		
GM steel-belted radial-ply tires	Avail.	Avail.	Avail.	Avail.	Avail.	Avail.	Avail.	Avail.	Avail.
White billboard lettered tires	Avail.	Avail.	Avail.	Avail.					
Engine block heater	Avail.	Avail.	Avail.	Avail.	Avail.	Avail.	Avail.	Avail.	Avail.
Heavy-duty air cleaner	Avail.	Avail.	Avail.	Avail.	Avail.	Avail.	Avail.	Avail.	Avail.
Heavy-duty Delcotron energizer	Avail.	Avail.	Avail.	Avail.	Avail.	Avail.	Std.	Std.	Std.
Maintenance-free energizer		Avail.	Avail.	Avail.	Avail.	Avail.	Avail.	Avail.	Avail.
Climate Control air conditioning	Avail.	Avail.	Avail.	Avail.	Avail.	Avail.	Avail.	Avail.	Avail.
Automatic Climate Control air conditioning						Avail.	Avail.	Avail.	Avail.
Special wheel covers	Avail.	Avail.	Avail.	Avail.	Avail.	Avail.	Avail.	Avail.	Avail.
Sun roof (coupes only)		Avail.	Avail.	Avail.		Avail.		Avail.	Avail.
Tilt steering wheel	Avail.	Avail.	Avail.	Avail.	Avail.	Avail.	Avail.	Avail.	Std.
Tilt and telescoping steering column						Avail.	Avail.	Avail.	Avail.
Electric trunk release		Avail.	Avail.	Avail.		Avail.		Avail.	Avail.
Electric door locks		Avail.	Avail.	Avail.	Avail.	Avail.	Avail.	Avail.	Avail.
Electric door and seatback locks (coupes only)						Avail.		Avail.	Avail.
Cruise Master speed control		Avail.	Avail.	Avail.	Avail.	Avail.	Avail.	Avail.	Avail.
Accessory group lights	Avail.	Avail.	Avail.	Avail.	Avail.	Avail.	Avail.	Avail.	Avail.
Low-fuel indicator						Avail.	Avail.	Avail.	Avail.
Special appearance and protection moldings	Avail.	Avail.	Avail.	Avail.	Avail.	Avail.	Avail.	Avail.	Avail.
Special steering wheels	Avail.	Avail.	Avail.	Avail.	Avail.	Avail.	Avail.		
Electric clock	Avail.	Avail.	Std.	Avail.	Avail.	Avail.	Avail.		
Electronic quartz-crystal-controlled digital clock						Avail.	Avail.	Std.	Std.
Power windows		Avail.	Avail.	Avail.	Avail.	Avail.	Avail.	Avail.	Avail.
Front fender-light monitors						Avail.	Avail.	Avail.	Avail.
Sport mirrors	Avail.	Avail.	Avail.	Avail.	Avail.	Avail.			Avail.
Remote-control outside rearview mirror (left)	Avail.	Avail.	Avail.	Avail.	Avail.	Avail.	Avail.	Std.	Std.
Remote-control outside rearview mirror (right)						Avail.	Avail.	Avail.	Avail.
Rear-window defogger (blower)	Avail.	Avail.	Avail.	Avail.		Avail.		Avail.	Avail.
Rear-window defogger (electric)		Avail.	Avail.	Avail.	Avail.	Avail.		Avail.	Avail.
Carpet savers and handi-mats	Avail.	Avail.	Avail.	Avail.	Avail.	Avail.	Avail.	Avail.	Avail.
Litter pocket		Avail.	Avail.	Avail.	Avail.	Avail.	Avail.	Avail.	Avail.
6-way power seat		Avail.	Avail.	Avail.	Avail.	Avail.	Avail.	Avail.	Avail.
Cornering lights						Avail.	Avail.	Avail.	Avail.
Speed alert		Avail.	Avail.	Avail.	Avail.	Avail.	Avail.	Avail.	Avail.
3-speed windshield wiper with low-speed delay feature						Avail.	Avail.	Avail.	Avail.
Soft Ray tinted glass	Avail.	Avail.	Avail.	Avail.	Avail.	Avail.	Avail.	Avail.	Avail.
Bumper guards	Avail.	Avail.	Avail.	Avail.	Std.	Std.	Std.	Avail.	Avail.
Outside thermometer						Avail.	Avail.	Avail.	Avail.
Convenience Center	Avail.	Avail.	Avail.	Avail.	Avail.	Avail.	Avail.	Avail.	Avail.
Full-length operating console		Avail.	Avail.	Avail.	Avail.				Avail.
Short, nonshift floor console		Avail.	Avail.	Avail.	Avail.				Avail.
AM radio, AM-FM radio	Avail.	Avail.	Avail.	Avail.	Avail.	Avail.	Avail.	Avail.	Avail.
AM-FM stereo radio with single front and rear speakers	Avail.								
Rear seat speaker (single)	Avail.	Avail.	Avail.	Avail.	Avail.	Avail.	Avail.	Avail.	Avail.
AM or AM-FM stereo radio and stereo tape player with front and rear dual speakers		Avail.	Avail.	Avail.	Avail.	Avail.	Avail.	Avail.	Avail.
AM-FM stereo radio with front and rear dual speakers		Avail.	Avail.	Avail.	Avail.	Avail.	Avail.	Avail.	Avail.
Front and rear dual speakers		Avail.	Avail.	Avail.	Avail.	Avail.	Avail.	Avail.	Avail.
Automatic power mast antenna						Avail.	Avail.	Avail.	Avail.

Avail.—Available   Std.—Standard

In Retrospect:
The History of Buick High Performance.

By Robert C. Ackerson

In the beginning of the automotive age, Buick was an active participant in motor sports and was driven in competition by such heroes of the time as "Wild" Bob Burman, Louis Chevrolet, his brother Gaston, and Ray Howard. The most famous of these early chariots of speed were the Buick Bugs, or to use their official names, the Buick 60 Specials. These cars were powered by 622 cubic inch, four-cylinder engines, weighed 2,600 lbs and were capable of lapping the Indianapolis track at speeds in excess of 105 mph.

These primordial racing Buicks and their considerable achievements were only dim reminders of a distant day to many modern Buick performance fans whose first exposure to a potent Buick was an encounter with a Gran Sport Skylark of the mid-sixties. But even these individuals were less than fully aware of the numerous Buick projects conducted since the early thirties that led to major advances in the performance of its production models.

An appropriate beginning point to establish as the origin of Buick's modern age of power is 1931, when the first Buick straight-eight engine was introduced. Five years later, in 1936, Buick placed in production the 320.2 cubic inch straight-eight that, along with a smaller version, served as the basis for its engine lineup until 1953 when the new V-8 was announced. The straight-eight was not noted for an ability to attain high rpm levels. Instead, its greatest virtue was its impressive low speed torque output.

By 1941, Buick was producing its straight-eights in two displacements of 320 and 248 cubic inches. The latter engine had first been introduced in 1934 for the new Series 40 (Special) series and had an additional quarter-inch added to its stroke in 1937. Its 3.093-inch bore and longer 4.125-inch stroke raised its displacement from 233 to 248 cubic inches. Buick did not, however, rely solely upon plenty of cubic inches for its performance reputation. Beyond the range of the general public's view were numerous activities involving the use of multiple carburetors that resulted in the use of

1931 Buick Model 64

BUICK DELIVERS THE GOODS

THERE are times when, more and more, cars are judged on how well they do a job—not on how many gadgets have been added to them.

Today it's the *net result* that counts—and so more stress is rightly placed on down-to-earth fundamentals such as power, economy, reliability.

How well Buick delivers the goods in this respect may be seen in its two most important engineering features—Buick FIREBALL design and Compound Carburetion.†

The FIREBALL engine is in tune with the times because it's built to get a higher percentage of usable power from every unit of fuel.

Its valve-in-head design makes it more efficient in the first place—a fact long recognized by builders of airplanes, racing cars and speedboats.

Add to it Buick's Dynaflash principle of combustion—which reaches an even higher degree of perfection through FIREBALL design—and you see why this great engine

reflects the modern trend toward *usefulness.*

Especially when linked with Compound Carburetion does Buick's engine satisfy today's demand for more power on less fuel.

Owners report that Buick's exclusive two-carburetor system not only makes driving more pleasurable but increases gasoline mileage as much as 10% to 15%—an item of growing importance in times when frugal use of fuel is being encouraged.

This policy of Buick's—to emphasize the things that count most—is important today and will be even more important tomorrow.

Nothing could be more appropriate for Buick to do right here and now than to pledge a continuance of that policy.

†Compound Carburetion is available on Buick SPECIAL models at slight additional cost; is standard on all other Series.

"Best Buick Yet"

EXEMPLAR OF GENERAL MOTORS VALUE

WHEN BETTER AUTOMOBILES ARE BUILT BUICK WILL BUILD THEM

McLouth stainless strip steel in the **automotive** industry

other applications

tubing

household

building

air-craft

McLouth

Harley J. Earl

1940 Y-Job

1953 Wildcat Show Car

1953 Skylark Convertible

Like a flight into tomorro

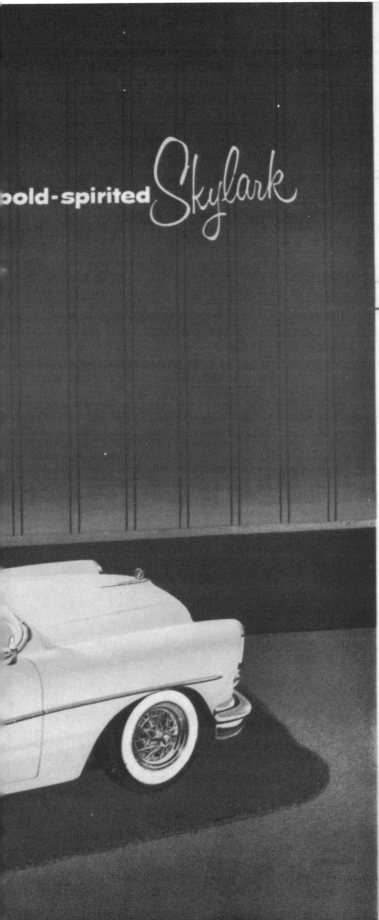

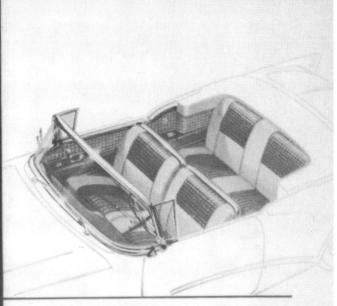

bold-spirited *Skylark*

THIS is the Buick for those with a boundless zest for automotive adventure.

This is the spirit-lifting Skylark—Buick's luxury sports car—with flight-designed lines, with road-snugging compactness, with the corsair-sweep of a finned rear deck—and with pulse-pounding performance second to no Buick ever built.

Rich with many of the "tomorrow" features of Buick's experimental car, the Wildcat—the Skylark stands just four feet, 11 inches high with the top up, is lavishly fitted with soft-tanned choice cowhide in four gorgeous color combinations, rolls on a low wire-wheeled 122-inch chassis.

As you would expect, this scintillating sportster is in limited production. As you would also expect, it has the mighty 200-horsepower Fireball V8 engine, Airpower Carburetor, 8.5 to 1 compression ratio, Twin-Turbine Dynaflow, Buick Safety Power Steering—plus, as additional standard equipment, Power Brakes, 4-way Power Seat, power-operated top and windows and telescopic antenna, Easy-Eye Glass, Selectronic Radio, WeatherWarden Heater and Defroster, and whitewall tires.

SKYLARK 2-Door 6-Passenger SPORTS CAR,
Model 100, 122-in. Wheelbase,
59 in. high with top up, 200 Horsepower

Compound Carburetion as standard equipment on all 1941 series except the Special. With 165 hp, the new Buicks were America's most powerful automobiles.

The positive impact this had upon the public's perception of Buick came on the heels of the publicity received by the Y-Job car which had been first shown in the spring of 1940. The Y-Job didn't make news because of its engine, which was standard, 320 cubic inch straight-eight. Instead, it stirred up a commotion because of its appearance which, since the Y-Job was regarded as a car of the future, told the public that cars with excitement in their lines weren't far away.

Although specific features of the Y-Job such as its grille, hood ornament and flowing fender shapes were to be common to the postwar Buicks, the use of Compound Carburetion was not resumed after the war. Production was first restricted to Super and Roadmaster models with the Special not joining the Buick line until November, 1946. The 248 cubic inch engine used for both the Special and Super lines developed 110 hp at 3600 rpms. The 320 cubic inch Roadmaster engine had a peak horsepower output of 144 at 3600 rpm.

Although the 1950 Super had a larger, 263 cubic inch engine equipped with hydraulic lifters that peaked at 128 hp at 3600 rpm, there was little in the way of exciting performance news coming from

Buick in the early fifties. One development that did attract a fair amount of attention was Buick's introduction of a four-barrel carburetor in 1952. Buick wasn't alone at General Motors with this innovation but, since it was a product of Buick research, it represented an important milestone in Buick's history.

Easily overshadowing the four-barrel's use was the double-barreled impact of two of the best known and, in some ways, most controversial, of General Motors' postwar dream cars, the LeSabre and the XP-300. Although the LeSabre was styled under the direct supervision of General Motors' styling boss, Harley Earl, the XP-300 was strictly a Buick styling exercise. More importantly, both cars were products of Buick engineering and thus provided additional evidence that behind Buick's somewhat conservative surface there was a mood and spirit of innovation and creativity.

The LeSabre was first shown to the public on December 29, 1950 and was almost immediately described as a forecast of the future. Neither Buick nor General Motors was the least bit shy about linking the LeSabre with the prewar Y-Job and one of the earliest press photos of the LeSabre showed it parked alongside the Y-Job. While much attention was attracted by the styling of the LeSabre and XP-300, their engines were equally worthy of close scrutiny. Under the direction of Charles Chayne,

From the 1957 full-line Catalogue

Buick launches a new kind of __instant__ performance

with a great new

VARIABLE PITCH DYNAFLOW

...and with an entirely new

V8 engine

to spark this performance

It's an actual fact that the 1957 Buick V8 is new from the crankshaft up.

To reduce its over-all dimensions to conform with Buick's low-sweep styling—yet increase Buick's power, compression and reserves—Buick engineers redesigned this V8's cylinder block, valves, valve ports, pistons, connecting rods, piston pins, and main bearings. Even the crankshaft was redesigned for greater strength.

So here you have 364 cubic inches of brand-new dynamite in a Buick V8 that's the most rugged, most powerful, smoothest and quietest of all time. 300 horsepower and 10.0 to 1 compression ratio in the ROADMASTER, SUPER and CENTURY. 250 horsepower and 9.5 to 1 in the SPECIAL. Highlighted here in detail are some of the advances found in these 1957 V8's and what they do—

A NEW AND BIGGER DEEP-FLANGE BLOCK — holds pistons, connecting rods, crankshaft and camshaft in rigid, smooth-running alignment for new record-high horsepower, and also provides increased cooling capacity.

A NEW AND BIGGER COMBUSTION CHAMBER centers each fuel charge compactly over the domed Power-Head piston at new record-high compression ratios for livelier, more efficient engine performance.

A NEW AND BIGGER BORE AND STROKE raise piston displacement to 364 cubic inches, providing capacity for record horsepower while retaining low stroke-to-bore ratio.

NEW AND BIGGER DOUBLE-Y EXHAUST MANIFOLDS conserve power for maximum road performance by relieving each cylinder of exhaust gases through widely separated branches, free from back-pressure and overlap.

1962 Special Convertible

Buick's chief engineer (who left Buick in 1951 to take charge of General Motors' engineering), his staff developed a 215 cubic inch, aluminum V-8 engine with a weight of 500 lbs that developed 335 hp at 5500 rpm and a compression ratio of 10.0:1. Two horizontal carburetors were fitted as were twin Roots-type superchargers. The use of such a high compression ratio in conjunction with supercharging was made possible by the inclusion of a dual fuel system. When the blowers were providing little or no boost, fuel was drawn from a tank filled with a high-octane gasoline. When boost increased, a supply of methanol was drawn into the fuel line.

The generally positive response to these dream cars, in addition to the growing acceptance of European sports cars in America, pointed the way to the Wildcat show car which toured the U.S. as part of the 1953 Motorama show. Although Buick described the Wildcat as "a single-seat sports

convertible of futuristic design," it was not destined to enter production as did the Corvette, which was also part of the Motorama display. Although the Wildcat's engine was a stock 188 hp, 322 cubic inch V-8, its suspension had several interesting features suggesting Buick was eager to explore ways of improving the roadability of its production models. For example, zero-degree caster, vertical kingpins were used at the front along with direct action shock absorbers. At the rear, the Wildcat's coil springs were joined by radius rods. A power steering unit was fitted that differed from the stock unit by having a faster 15:1, rather than the stock 23:1 ratio.

The Wildcat wasn't the only way that Buick celebrated its fiftieth anniversary. Of at least equal importance was the introduction of the first Skylark model in June, 1953. This $4,596 convertible was described as a "six-passenger sports car" by Buick which raised the ire of more than a few dyed-in-the-wool sports car enthusiasts. The Skylark used standard Roadmaster components but achieved a look of its own by virtue of full cut-out wheel openings, a notched beltline, lower windshield height and Kelsey-Hayes wire wheels. The following year, a second edition of the Skylark was offered on the 118-inch wheelbase Century chassis.

In spite of the strong performance of its V-8 powered models, Buick usually wasn't a subject discussed in any depth by American publications devoted to sports cars. That condition changed in 1958 when Buick installed as standard equipment on all its series, except the Specials, new aluminum-finned front brakes. These had first been used in 1957 for the Roadmaster 75. In an era when Buick's styling was, in the view of even its most avid supporters, gaudy and ostentatious, it had the best brakes of any American passenger car. Reflecting this was the special award "Sports Cars Illustrated" presented to Buick "in recognition of outstanding and significant contribution in the automotive field . . . for major advance in brakes."

Compared to ordinary iron drums, Buick's aluminum alloy front brakes dissipated heat to its outer surface three times faster. In addition, the fins created an air turbulence that came into contact with the larger than normal surface area. The result was, in the view of "Sports Cars Illustrated" (February, 1958), brakes whose performance was "as

significant today as Oldsmobile's V-8 engine was in 1949."

During the years when Buick's V-8s were honed to a sharp performance edge, the V-6 engine, which had first been used in 1962 for the Special, received scant attention from supercar fans. In 1970, it was replaced in the Buick engine lineup by Chevrolet's 250 cubic inch inline six and its tooling was sold to American Motors. A few years later, in 1974, the entire American automobile industry, not to mention the supercars, was in deep trouble and, as a means to improve its product's fuel economy, Buick bought back from AMC the production line for the V-6 and offered it for the 1975 model year.

At that point, it was hard to believe that the Buick V-8 engine would be out of production in five years and the V-6 would be refined and developed into an engine worthy of installation in Buicks that would be highly respectable performers. This evolution began in earnest in 1976, when, for the second consecutive year, Buick provided the pace car for the Indianapolis 500. Although Buick offered a total of 1,290 Centurys with a pace car paint scheme, the actual pace car had no direct production counterpart. Its role in setting the pace for the modern Buick performance car was, however, tremendous since it was a clear signal that Buick was determined to acquire an expertise with

1976 Century Custom Indy Pace Car

Buick 1976: The Free Spirit of the Indianapolis 500

Buick has been chosen as the Official Pace Car for the 1976 Indianapolis 500-Mile Race which is scheduled for Sunday, May 30, 1976. This year's Pace Car is a specially prepared silver, orange, red and black 1976 Buick Century Custom. Pace Car features include customized roof panels, body striping and monogramming.

1979 Riviera

relatively small turbocharged engines to make them exciting powerplants.

The Indy car was fitted with a Rajay turbocharger, a specially calibrated four-barrel carburetor, modified ignition system, forged aluminum pistons and reworked cylinder heads and cam. The result was a true horsepower output in the vicinity of 330 and a car capable of speeds above the 130 mph mark.

In 1978, Buick was ready to offer the public a production model V-6 with an AiResearch turbocharger and 165 hp that could be ordered for either the Regal Sport Coupe or the LeSabre Coupe. Adding to its appeal was the V-6's even-firing feature.

The next year, a totally restyled and downsized Riviera was introduced with specifications that included all-independent suspension, front-wheel drive, optional four-wheel disk brakes and a turbocharged V-6 engine. No wonder "Road & Track" March, 1979, commented that "if General Motors had given us the specifications of the 1979 Buick Riviera five years ago and said they were going to build the car we probably would have fallen off our

chairs." With 185 hp and 280 lb-ft coming from the 231 cubic inch V-6, the Riviera was capable of 0 to 60 mph runs in less than 10 seconds.

The new Riviera was not just a quick car that received its get-up-and-go fron a refined, small displacement engine. Instead, it was the leading edge of a new generation of performance Buicks that combine traditional Buick virtues with a performance mode that has a definite European flavor. Nowhere is this seen more clearly than in the latest models. The new Somerset Regal, for example, has a three-liter V-6 with multiport fuel injection that weighs just 50 lbs more than the standard 2.5-liter four-cylinder and develops 125 hp at 4800 rpm.

In all series above the Somerset, Buick offers T-Type versions that combine turbocharged V-6 engines with numerous performance components, giving them superior driving characteristics. The flagships of this fleet of rapid Buicks are the Regal Grand National and the Riviera T-Type. Both cars have 3.8-liter V-6 turbocharged engines equipped with sequential port fuel injection that produce 200 hp. Complementing this high output is a special Gran Touring suspension that consists of higher

1985 BUICK SOMERSET REGAL   3.0 MFI (F41)

PERFORMANCE

ACCELERATION

Time to distance, sec:
- 0-100 ft 4.2
- 0-500 ft 10.4
- 0-1320 ft (¼ mi) 18.6
- Speed at end of ¼ mi ... 76 mph

Time to speed, sec:
- 0-30 .... 4.3
- 0-50 .... 8.6
- 0-60 .... 11.7

ACCELERATION (graph: Distance in feet vs Elapsed time in seconds)

HP/TORQUE (graph: 3.0 MFI TORQUE / 3.0 MFI HP)

HANDLING*

- Max lateral accel, g .... .76
- Roll gain ..... 5.7 degrees per g
- Steering sensitivity ... 1.18g per 100 degrees of steering wheel angle

*One car sample

POWERTRAIN

ENGINE 3.0 Litre MFI V-6

- Type .... Buick-Bosch multiport fuel injected with electronic mass air flow system 90° V6 arrangement, computer controlled coil ignition and mass air flow sensor - designed underhood appearance.
- Valve Arrangement .... Overhead Valve with individual Rocker Pedestals
- Bore & Stroke (In.) 3.8x2.66
- Displacement (cu.in.) 3.0L (181)
- Cylinder Head & Block Material .... Cast Iron
- Compression Ratio 9.0:1
- Net/Installed Horsepower & Engine RPM .... 125 @ 4900
- Net/Installed Torque (lb-ft) & Engine RPM .... 150 @ 2400
- Recommended Fuel ..... No-lead Reg.
- Fuel System Type .... Port Fuel Injection
- EPA Projected Fuel Estimated (Adjusted):
  - -City 20
  - -Hwy 26

DRIVETRAIN

- Transmission
  - Type .... 3-spd automatic with Torque Conv. clutch
  - Selector Pattern PRND21
- Gear Ratio
  - First 2.84
  - Second 1.57
  - Third 1.00
  - Reverse (R) 2.07
- Max Ratio at Stall (torque converter) .. 2.35
- Cooling .... Water
- Total Oil Capacity 8.5L
  - Drain & Refill (pts) 18
- Final Drive Ratio 2.84

DIMENSIONS

	COUPE
EXTERIOR	
Length	180.0
Width	66.6
Height	52.1
Wheelbase	103.4
Front Tread	55.5
Rear Tread	55.2
INTERIOR (Front)	
Leg Room	42.9
Head Room	37.7
Shoulder Room	53.7
Hip Room	51.9
(Rear)	
Leg Room	34.3
Head Room	36.9
Shoulder Room	55.4
Hip Room	50.7
TRUNK	
Luggage Capacity (ft³)	13.6
FUEL TANK	
Refill (Capacity gals)	13.6
WEIGHT	
Est. Base Curb (lbs)	2542

ate springs, front and rear stabilizer bars, faster
steering, and a performance rear axle ratio.

Buick did not base its performance models upon
a narrow foundation. In the age of the straight-
eight, it marketed cars that used that engine's
virtues to the utmost. Later came the era of the large
displacement V-8 and the Buick versions were
among the best. Today, Buick is a leader in the
development of automobiles that combine the best
of the past with the best of today's technology, to
which is added just a glimpse of the future. The
result makes the old Buick slogan, "When better cars
are built, Buick will build them," more exciting than
ever.

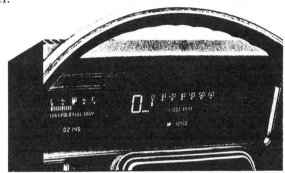

A COMMITMENT TO TECHNICAL EXCELLENCE

Buick's new computer-controlled Electronic Instrument Cluster is strong evidence of Buick's commitment to becoming an industry leader in the use of microprocessing technology in automobiles.

The expanded fuel gage and sophisticated multi-gage are unique to Buick. And the eight-bit microprocessor used to control the system is capable of updating the display information 125 times per second.

This Electronic Instrument Cluster responds directly to consumer demands for high technology graphic displays in their automobiles. It's no surprise that it comes from Buick.

1985 Somerset Regal Coupe

Buicks in Print: The High Performance Literature.

Buick's endeavors in the performance arena were well-covered in the Buick sales literature of the sixties and seventies. Buick, as all true performance buffs know, built some of the best-handling, best-balanced of the muscle era cars and it is only right that they should have been commemorated in the literature of the time.

the new Buick sizzlers

Buick wanted the whole world to know they were serious about performance when they issued the catalogue whose cover appears above. The "Buick Sizzlers" really did sizzle, but no more so than the cover of this catalogue—one of the best graphic efforts to come out of Detroit ad agencies during the sixties.

There were three, count 'em, three, Buick sizzlers in 1965. Left to right, they were the Riviera Gran Sport, the Wildcat and the Skylark Gran Sport—the car many regard as the best all-around musclecar from this era (page 66).

Riviera GS

Performance options: Ride and handling kit (extra-quick, 15:1 power steering, plus heavy-duty springs and shocks). Chromed steel wheels. Everything else is built in as regular equipment.

Comfort, convenience, and appearance options: Power windows, power vent windows, power seat. Air conditioning, tinted glass. AM and AM/FM radios, electric antenna, rear seat speaker. Rear window defroster. Remote control rear-view mirror. Automatic trunk release. Whitewall tires.

Engine:

	Standard
Bhp @ rpm	360 @ 4400
Torque, lb-ft. @ rpm	465 @ 2800
Type	ohv V-8
Displacement, cu. in.	425
Bore and stroke	4.31 x 3.64
Carburetion	2-4BBL
Compression ratio	10.25:1

Short-stroke 90° V-8, cast iron alloy block, with five main bearings. Intake valves — 1.875″. Exhaust valves —1.50″. Low-restriction dual exhausts.

Transmission: A 3-speed torque convertor automatic is standard, its shift lever mounted in a console. Ratios are 2.48, 1.48, and 1.00:1, with a total torque multiplication of 5.50:1. No other transmissions are available.

Axle ratios:

Engine	Transmission	Standard Axle Ratio	Special Order Axle Ratios	
360 bhp	Automatic	3.42	3.23	3.58

Suspension: Ball joint independent front, three-link rear. Coil springs, front and rear. Heavy-duty springs and shocks are available as part of the optional ride and handling package, which also includes an extra-quick power steering ratio of 15:1.

Steering: Power steering of the recirculating ball bearing type is regular equipment. Ratio —17.5:1. An extra-quick, 15:1 power steering ratio is available as part of the optional ride and handling package, which also includes heavy-duty springs and shocks.

Brakes: Hydraulic, duo-servo, internal expanding, self-adjusting. Drums are 12″ finned aluminum, front; 12″ finned cast iron, rear. Swept area —320.5 sq. in.

Dimensions and capacities: Wheelbase is 117 inches. Tread is 60.2 inches front, 59 inches rear. Overall length is 209 inches. Overall width is 77.0 inches. Height is 52.1 inches. The gas tank holds approximately 20 gallons.

Wildcat

Performance options: 340-bhp, 4BBL engine. 360-bhp, 2-4BBL engine. 4-speed transmission. Heavy-duty springs and shocks. Limited-slip differential. Tachometer. Chromed steel wheels.

Comfort, convenience, and appearance options: Super Turbine automatic transmission. Power steering, power brakes, power windows, power seat. Air conditioning, tinted glass. AM and AM/FM radios, electric antenna, rear seat speaker (except Conv.). Console. Windshield washers and 2-speed electric wipers. Tilting steering wheel (except with manual steering or manual transmission). Cornering lights, back-up lights, trunk light, parking brake warning light. Glare-proof mirror. Automatic trunk release. Electric clock. Remote control rear-view mirror. Whitewall tires. Rear window defroster (except Conv.).

Engines:

	Standard	Optional*	Optional*
Bhp @ rpm	325 @ 4400	340 @ 4400	360 @ 4400
Torque, lb-ft. @ rpm	445 @ 2800	465 @ 2800	465 @ 2800
Type	ohv V-8	ohv V-8	ohv V-8
Displacement, cu. in.	401	425	425
Bore and stroke	4.19 x 3.64	4.31 x 3.64	4.31 x 3.64
Carburetion	4BBL	4BBL	2-4BBL
Compression ratio	10.25:1	10.25:1	10.25:1

Short-stroke 90° V-8, cast iron alloy block, with five main bearings. Intake valves —1.875″. Exhaust valves —1.50″. Low-restriction dual exhausts standard on 360-bhp engine, optional on others.
*Not available with 3-speed manual transmission.

Transmissions: The standard transmission is a 3-speed, its shift lever mounted on the steering column. Ratios are 2.49, 1.59, and 1.00:1. A close-ratio 4-speed is available, its shift lever mounted on the floor. Ratios are 2.20, 1.64, 1.31, and 1.00:1. Also available is a 3-speed torque convertor automatic with a column shift —or, at extra cost, with its shift lever mounted in a console. Ratios are 2.48, 1.48, and 1.00:1, with a total torque multiplication of 5.50:1.

Axle ratios:

Engine	Transmission	Standard Axle Ratio	Special Order Axle Ratios			
325 bhp	3- or 4-speed	3.42	3.23	3.58	3.91	
	Automatic	3.07	2.78	3.36	3.42	3.58
340 and	4-speed	3.42	3.23	3.58	3.91	
360 bhp	Automatic	3.07	2.78	3.36	3.42	3.58

Suspension: Ball joint independent front, four-link rear. Coil springs, front and rear. Heavy-duty springs and shocks are available on special order.

Steering: Recirculating ball bearing steering gear. Manual ratio —28:1. Power steering ratio —17.5:1.

Brakes: Hydraulic, duo-servo, internal expanding, self-adjusting. Drums are 12″ finned aluminum, front; 12″ finned cast iron, rear. Swept area —320.5 sq. in.

Dimensions and capacities: Wheelbase is 126 inches. Tread is 63.4 inches front, 63 inches rear. Overall length is 219.8 inches. Overall width is 80 inches. Height is 55.2 inches. The gas tank holds approximately 25 gallons.

Skylark GS

Performance options: Close-ratio 4-speed transmission. Limited-slip differential. Tachometer. Chromed steel wheels.

Comfort, convenience, and appearance options: Super Turbine automatic transmission. Power steering, power brakes, power windows, power seat. Air conditioning, tinted glass. Radio, rear seat speaker (except Conv.). Console, consolette. Windshield washers and 2-speed electric wipers. Tilting steering wheel (except with manual steering or manual transmission). Back-up lights, trunk light. Glare-proof mirror. Electric clock. Remote control rear-view mirror. Whitewall tires. Rear window defroster (except Conv.).

Engine:

	Standard
Bhp @ rpm	325 @ 4400
Torque, lb-ft. @ rpm	445 @ 2800
Type	ohv V-8
Displacement, cu. in.	400
Bore and Stroke	4.19 x 3.64
Carburetion	4BBL
Compression ratio	10.25:1

Short-stroke 90 V-8, cast iron alloy, with five main bearings. Intake valves — 1.875″. Exhaust valves —1.50″. Low-restriction dual exhausts.

Transmissions: The standard transmission is a floor-shift 3-speed with all forward gears synchronized. Ratios are 2.42, 1.61, and 1.00:1. A close-ratio 4-speed is available, its shift lever mounted on the floor. Ratios are 2.20, 1.64, 1.31, and 1.00:1. Also available is a 2-speed torque convertor automatic, its shift lever mounted in a console. Ratios are 1.76 and 1.00, with a total torque multiplication of 4.32:1.

Axle ratios:

Engine	Transmission	Standard Axle Ratio	Special Order Axle Ratios				
325 bhp	3- or 4-speed	3.36	3.08	3.55	3.73		
	Automatic	3.08	2.78	3.23	3.36	3.55	3.73

Suspension: Ball joint independent front, four-link rear. Coil springs, front and rear. Heavy-duty springs, shocks, and stabilizer bar —designed specifically for the Skylark GS —are regular equipment.

Steering: Recirculating ball bearing steering gear. Manual ratio —24:1. Power steering ratio —17.5:1.

Brakes: Hydraulic, duo-servo, internal expanding, self-adjusting. Drums are 9.5″ cast iron, front and rear. Swept area —268.6 sq. in.

Dimensions and capacities: Wheelbase is 115 inches. Tread is 58 inches, front and rear. Overall length is 203.4 inches. Overall width is 73.9 inches. Height is 53.5 inches. The gas tank holds approximately 20 gallons.

Introducing the tuned car. 1966 Buick.

THE MACHINES. BUICK GS-340. BUICK GS-400.

BUICK '68

Here are the ways Buick talks your language in 1968.

GS⊠BY BUICK!

Buick never went out for brute strength like most of its competitors in the muscle era, preferring to balance power with finesse. Many observers thought the Buick approach the most satisfying of all, and Buick ad men decided to promote the approach in the 1966 literature. The cover of the saver catalogue appears at left above.

Somehow you get the impression that the catalogue, whose cover is shown at left center, covers the Buick GS-340 and GS-400 . . . The Machines. This catalogue is probably the second-best Buick performance effort of all time, from a graphics viewpoint. Only the 1965 "Buick Sizzlers" catalogue exceeds it.

The 1968 Buick literature was long on pictures and short on text. The cover described it pretty well, It was, indeed, the 1968 Buick catalogue (shown at left below). The GS-400 spread, reproduced on pages 68 and 69, is typical.

The GSX has come to be one of the most sought-after of all the high performance Buicks of the muscle era. It is prized for its special blend of power and handling. And, it was affordable, too. The cover of the exclusive GSX brochure is shown above.

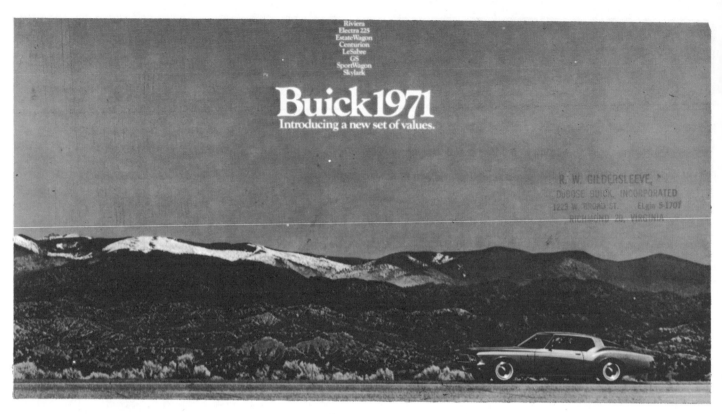

By 1971, performance was, if not dead, certainly going fast. The Buick Riviera, barely discernible in the mountain landscape on the catalogue cover (shown above) and new for 1971, was distinguished, or at least notable, for its psuedo-boattail rear end, known in some circles as Bill Mitchell's Revenge. It is hard to tell if the car illustrated is a Gran Sport, but a GS Riviera was still listed in the catalogue that year.

Since they began, the T-Types have received ample coverage in the regular Buick literature. In 1983, however, they achieved something special with a catalogue of their own. Five flavors were featured: Century, Skyhawk, Skylark, Regal (before it went black-out) and Riviera. The cover is shown below.

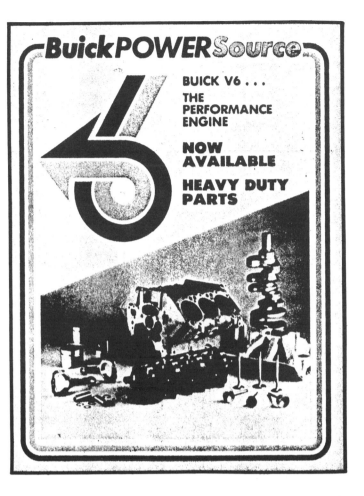

Buick has been in the forefront of V-6 technology. By the time the folder (shown at left) was issued in 1984, the division had started selling heavy-duty engine components. The "Buick Power Source" brochure featured both Stage I and Stage II equipment, along with the customary warning that these parts were intended for "Off Highway" use only. Customers were solemnly advised that Federal law prohibited their use on the street. And that, of course, settled that . . .

BUICK

The Regal T-Type went black-out in 1984 and this two-sided color sheet, shown at right and below, was issued to commemorate the event.

Buick Gran Sports: An Advertising Portfolio.

BUICK MOTOR DIVISION

Superbird.

The Skylark Gran Sport.
400 cu. in. / 325 bhp.
Bucket seats.
Floor-shift, all-synchro 3 speed.
Heavy-duty suspension.
Oversized, 7.75 x 14 tires.
Performance axle ratios.
Zow!
The Buick Skylark
Gran Sport

The Riviera with muscles on its muscles.
New Riviera Gran Sport.

There has always been
a vast body of admirers who wouldn't
change a hair on the normal Riviera's chest
for the world. But we have discovered, lurking
in the wings, a cluster of hotbloods who secretly have been
yearning for a little more heat. Thus, the Riviera Gran Sport.
It packs a 425-cubic inch, 360-hp, V-8 with 465 lb-ft of
torque. (Numbers were never lovelier.) And we went behind
the firewall, too. A limited-slip differential. Power-assisted
brakes and steering. And you can specify the heavy-duty set
of springs, shocks and stabilizer bar. What happens when
you put everything together is the most exciting automobile
to travel any road. Wouldn't you really rather have a Buick?

One of the new Gran Sports from Buick

BUICK MOTOR DIVISION

There are Buicks that would rattle your faith in the established order of sporting machinery. The Skylark GS, for one.

Notch-back seats that convert into semi-buckets are standard. Bucket seats are available.

A tachometer is available.

The standard engine. Bhp—325 @ 4400. Torque—445 lb-ft @ 2800.

More engine. Extra cost. Bhp—340 @ 4600. Torque—445 lb-ft @ 3200. Carburetion—Quadrajet 4BBL.

Chromed-steel 14-inch wheels are available. Choice of 7.75 x 14 red-line or whitewall tires at no extra cost. Axle ratios: 2.78, 2.93, 3.36, 3.55, 3.90. 4.30:1 (special order). Positive Traction is included with all performance axles, at extra cost.

The following safety equipment is standard on all Buicks: 2-speed electric wipers and windshield washer; padded dash; padded sun visors; back-up lights; shatter-resistant rear-view mirror; outside rear-view mirror; and front and rear seat belts (which we sure wish you'd buckle).

Floor-shift all-synchro 3-speed standard. Automatic and close-ratio 4-speed are available.

Heavy-duty springs, shocks, stabilizer bar, and frame are standard. Metallic brake linings and a rear stabilizer bar are available, dealer installed.

1966 Buick.
The tuned car.

The extra-strong 425-cubic incher. Bhp—360 @ 4400. Torque—465 lb-ft @ 2800. Carburetion—2x4 BBL. The standard engine has 340 bhp, the same torque, the same inches, and 1x4 BBL.

Bench and bucket seats are both standard; your choice. Included among the standard safety features are seat belts, front and rear; a second to buckle them could add years to your life.

Super Turbine automatic transmission is standard, as are power steering (with tilting steering wheel) and power brakes.

Chromed-steel wheels are available. A limited-slip differential is standard, with a choice of axle ratios. Red-line or whitewall tires are both standard; your choice.

Heavy-duty springs and shocks are standard. An extra-quick, 15:1 power steering gear is available.

Isn't it about time you stopped playing automobile and started driving the real thing?   Buick Riviera GS.

Buick talks the language of people who want a car that makes the world sit up and take notice.

GS 350 has a 350 CID V8 that delivers 280 horsepower @ 4600 rpm. 375 pounds feet of torque @ 3200 rpm. It's connected to a 3-speed stick that's synchronized in all forward gears. Heavy-duty 3- or 4-speed floor-mounted transmissions with Hurst shifters are available. Or you can order a Super Turbine 300 automatic that's as tough as it ought to be.

More? A long list of GM safety equipment is standard. Everything from seat back latches to side marker lights.

1968 Advertisement

BUICK MOTOR DIVISION   MARK OF EXCELLENCE

GS 350 has a new 112-inch wheelbase and
59-inch front track that makes it a true
Gran Sport. The sportier a Buick looks,
the sportier it acts.

You can add even more.
A high performance rear axle.
And suspension system. A choice of rallye kits.
GS 350 offers as much more as you'd like.

Now wouldn't you really rather have the car
that talks your language? 1968 Buick.

Buick's GSX.
A limited edition.

• 455-4 Engine (350 Horsepower) • Tachometer-hood mounted • Special Rallye Steering Wheel • Power Front Disc Brakes • 4-speed Manual Transmission • 3.42 axle ratio with Positive Traction Differential • G60-15 Billboard Wide Oval Tires • Special Front Stabilizer Bar • Front and Rear Spoilers • Bucket Seats (Black) • Heavy duty front & rear shocks • Rear Stabilizer Bar • Rear Control Arms & Bushings • Firm Ride Rear Springs • GSX Ornamentation.

Another light-your-fire car from Buick.

GM

MARK OF EXCELLENCE

Light your fire.

BUICK MOTOR DIVISION

Warm up to one of the light-your-fire Buicks,
the 1970 Buick GS 455 Stage I.
What is Stage I? It begins with a modified version of Buick's new
455 cubic-inch V8. It gets you a high-lift cam, a big Quadrajet carburetor, a
low-restriction dual exhaust system, heavy-duty valve springs and cooling system,
even functional hood scoops. It delivers 360 horsepower, 510 foot/pounds of torque.
After more?
You can order an extra heavy-duty Rallye suspension with front and rear
track bars. You can add G60x15 super wide ovals, front disc brakes and replace
the standard three-speed manual transmission with a specially-calibrated
Turbo-Hydramatic or floor-mounted, Hurst-linked four-speed manual.
The 1970 Buick GS 455 Stage I. It's the enthusiast's machine
you've been asking us to build.
Consider it built.

Now, wouldn't you really rather have a Buick.

Buick's Gentleman's Cruiser: A Brief History of the Riviera.

By R. Perry Zavitz

The following text is excerpted from, "Riviera: A Classic Source Book," also published by Bookman Publishing. It is one of the best sources for selected reproductions of original factory literature pertaining to the Riviera and includes detailed commentary about options, prices, specifications and important historical notes.

The name Riviera is almost synonymous with Buick, even though it was used about a decade earlier by the tiny American Bantam convertible. The first Buick Riviera was a mid-year introduction in the spring of 1949—a new and stylish car described as a hardtop convertible.

Built on the top-line Roadmaster chassis, this Riviera had a permanent steel roof, but no center posts. With the windows rolled down, the Riviera was as open (except for the roof) as a convertible. This idea was not a Buick origination, but it was Buick that made it a success. The hardtop was a North American phenomenon and Buick was its prime mover.

So popular was the initial Roadmaster Riviera, that Buick added several Rivieras to its 1950 range. A hardtop was added to the middle-line Super series, as well as longer, more luxurious four-door sedans in the Super and Roadmaster lines. They were all called Rivieras. Then a Riviera hardtop was added to the lower Special series for 1951.

The next logical move for the hardtop was to extend the same idea to the four-door body. So, Buick led the way in mass-producing four-door hardtops in 1955 on the Century and Special and, in 1956, in all its lines. These too were called Rivieras.

When all Buick model series names were changed on the 1959 models, the Riviera name survived, but in a very restricted area. There was only one Riviera. It was one of the two four-door hardtops offered in the top-line Electra 225 series—the hardtop with six side windows. If there was any price difference between these two hardtops from 1959 to 1962, the Riviera was the more expensive.

An entirely new car—something unlike any Buick before—was introduced for 1963. It was categorized as a personal luxury car. Abundant power was featured. This Buick continued the Riviera name (which was used from 1949 to 1958 on all its hardtops regardless of series, and from 1959 to 1962 on the top-of-the-line Electra 225 four-door hardtop).

The new Riviera was a two-door hardtop, a body type usually referred to at this time by General Motors as a Sport Coupe. No other body types were offered by Riviera. Its styling was vastly different from any other Buick. An indication of its level of luxury, and the willingness of buyers to pay extra for luxury options, is the fact that 19,880 Rivieras were equipped with $430 optional air-conditioning. That was 49.7%.

1951 Super Riviera Hardtop Convertible

LIMITED 4-Door 6-Passenger RIVIERA,
Model 750, 127½-in. Wheelbase, 300 Horsepower

ROADMASTER 75 4-Door 6-Passenger RIVIERA,
Model 75, 127½-in. Wheelbase, 300 Horsepower

Riviera used a 117-inch wheelbase, which was six inches shorter than LeSabre and Wildcat, yet five inches more than Skylark. This car was no lightweight, tipping the scales at an even two tons, but it was significantly lighter than the hot Wildcat. It used the same motor—the 401 cubic inch 325 hp V-8 of the Wildcat and Electra.

Performance of the 1963 Riviera was as outstanding as its other characteristics. The "World Car Catalog" gave its top speed as 121 mph. That meant it had a slight edge on the Wildcat's 120 maximum mph.

Production was a substantial 40,000 for its freshman model year. The Riviera did not take long in getting itself known in the marketplace. Its $4,333 price tag, in the 1963 economy, did not seem to be a deterrent to the car's acceptance.

Very few styling differences were to be found on the 1964 Riviera (the oval "R" symbol was added here and there), but there was an engine change. A new 425 cubic inch V-8 that developed 340 hp was standard. (Only the Chrysler 300-K had a more powerful standard engine that year.) But Riviera offered an optional version. Costing $140 extra, it was the same engine but with two four-barrel carburetors instead of one. That boosted the output to 360 hp, a rating exceeded only by three other optional 1964 engines (Corvette and Chrysler 300-K).

That generous boost in power, along with a slight reduction in weight, gave the Riviera, with the two-carb option, a power-to-weight ratio of just under 11 lbs per hp. In standard form, the Riviera's maximum speed was 128 mph and the standing quarter mile time was 16.2 seconds, so claimed the "World Car Catalog." Those 24 extra cubic inches in the engine, and the 15 to 35 more horses they produced, clearly made a difference in the Riviera's performance.

A slight revision to the front of the Riviera, mainly the disappearing headlights, gave the 1965 model a very distinctive appearance. It was one of the best-looking Rivieras ever. However, the car grew an inch and added some 85 lbs for a total weight of 4,036 lbs.

Under the hood, some changes were made as well, but one of them was a retrograde step. The standard engine was the 401 cubic inch motor used two seasons earlier. Its output was not modified, so 325 hp was its rating. Optional, though, were the same super-power motors of 1964. The buyer could choose either the single four-barrel carburetor, 425 cubic inch 340 hp V-8 for $48, or the dual-carb version costing $188 and developing 360 hp, as before.

Performance-wise, the "World Car Catalog" claimed top speed was 129, 131 and 133 mph for the 325, 340 and 360 hp engines, respectively.

There was a Gran Sport option available in 1965 for the first time on the Riviera. It consisted of the 360 hp engine with its dual carburetors and dual exhausts, high-performance 3.42 rear axle (3.23 was standard) with positive traction differential, and special wheel covers.

Heavy-duty suspension was available optionally, but that was not part of the Gran Sport package. Another option, air-conditioning, was installed in a growing number of Rivieras. A total of 24,038, or 69.5%, had it.

A new body enveloped the 1966 Riviera. Actually, it shared the same basic body of the new Oldsmobile Toronado, but retained its own rear-wheel-drive chassis. Wheelbase was stretched two inches, and overall length grew three inches. Its avoirdupois increased 144 lbs, making it a 4,180 lb car.

There was only one engine obtainable in the 1966 Riviera. It was the 340 hp single carburetor 425 cubic inch engine. There were no other choices, at least from the factory. However, the buyer could order the two-carburetor version for $255. It was a dealer-installed option that increased output to 360 hp.

Several magazines tested the 1966 Riviera. "Mechanix Illustrated's" Tom McCahill got the best 0 to 60 acceleration time of 6.8 seconds and with the 340 hp engine. Quarter-mile acceleration by "Motor Trend" was 16.4 seconds and 84 mph with the single carb motor. "Car and Driver," using a twin-carb car, did it in 15.9 seconds and 87 mph. McCahill clocked a top speed of 125, but he thought a good carburetor setup would help the Riviera reach 130. That agrees with the "World Car Catalog" maximum speed of 129

1965 Riviera Gran Sport

mph.

"Road & Track" naturally praised the $177 Gran Sport option. By this time, the GS package did include high-performance springs and shocks, along with Positraction rear axle.

Of course, many other options were available on the Riviera. One of the most popular was air-conditioning, which actually dropped slightly in price to $421. There were 33,950 of the 1966 Rivieras equipped with that option, or 74.9%. Power windows were slightly more popular. There were 78.6%, or 35,633 which had that convenience. Power seats were installed in 23,672—63.2%. Positraction differential-equipped 1966 Rivieras amounted to 12,412. That was 27.4%, but such

installations diminished each year thereafter. However, cruise control was a growing option. Just 7,388—16.3% of the 1966 models had it, but the percentage would increase annually. The fastest-growing option was a vinyl roof. A mere 3,284 had this appearance feature in 1966—just 7.2%. But the popularity of this appearance option would explode.

The base list price for the Riviera was set at $4,424. Production for the 1966 Riviera shot up almost 11,000 to a 45,348 total. That made the Riviera Buick's most popular model for the year. One of the reasons for the increased demand for the 1966 Riviera was the fact that it was frequently featured in Buick magazine advertising.

With little difference in appearance for 1967, the

1970 Riviera

1971. Buick introduces a new set of values.

1971 Buick Riviera GS.

BUICK MOTOR DIVISION

The things people expected out of a performance car a few years ago aren't the same anymore.

They want more than emblems in return for their money. They want more value.

And value is what has led more people to Buick's performance cars every year. A whole new set of values await you in your dealer's showroom now.

Our new Riviera GS is the ultimate in an American luxury performance car. Its styling alone will set a trend. But you want more than that. And we want to give you more.

The Riviera engine.
The new Riviera GS features a big 455 cubic-inch V-8 engine designed to run clean and smooth. We put in improvements like a new time-modulated carburetor choke that will give quicker warm-ups and a more consistent fuel mixture. And we've even added new, exclusive nickel-plated engine exhaust valves for smoother engine operation and longer valve life.

The transmission.
A specially calibrated 3-speed Turbo-Hydramatic 400. The shift lever can be mounted on an available between-the-seats console that is slanted toward the driver for ease of operation.

Suspension and handling.
New, longer wheelbase with improved AccuDrive directional stability system. Full-perimeter frame. Heavy, side-guard beams for added protection. A four-link rear suspension, specifically engineered fiberglass belted, white wall tires, heavy-duty springs and shocks, stabilizer bars and heavy-duty suspension bushings will give you ride and handling without peer. Positive traction differential (3.42 axle ratio standard).

The interior and braking.
More room inside. Even in the trunk. Driver cockpit includes new control center designed around driver for ease and convenience. New brakes have a unique valve that proportions braking force front to rear to help give you quick, smooth, straight-line stops. Standard equipment includes power front disc brakes, more nimble variable-ratio power steering and, of course, automatic transmission.

MaxTrac. Another Buick first.
We introduced MaxTrac for 1971. And you can order it for the Riviera. Listen to what it does. If you're on the ice or in the snow or in the rain, MaxTrac helps give you cat-like handling ability. A miniature on-board computer does it by controlling the power to the rear wheels to reduce slipping on slick surfaces.

One last point. Study a new Riviera GS in person at your Buick dealer's. Only a Buick Dealer can offer you our new set of values. And we want you to test them against your values. We say we build cars that are something to believe in. So, ask a lot of questions. Until there is only one question left.

Wouldn't you really rather have a Buick.

Something to believe in.

**1972 Riviera Silver Arrow III
Experimental Show Car**

Riviera did have a difference under the hood. A new and larger motor was standard. It displaced 430 cubic inches, had a single four-barrel carburetor and developed 360 hp. There was very little increase in overall weight, so the increased power was not lost. There was no optional power choice, either from the factory or the dealer.

Actually, there was little need for more potent engine options. Riviera's motor was larger than any other that year, except Cadillac and certain Chrysler, Dodge and Plymouth models. Furthermore, the Riviera's engine had the highest horsepower rating of any standard 1967 engine.

In a comparison test with the Eldorado,

1973 Riviera

Toronado, Grand Prix and Thunderbird, Motor Trend found the Riviera gave the fastest in the 0 to 60 acceleration time. It took 7.8 seconds. Speed at the end of a standing quarter-mile was 86 mph for the Riviera. That was a tie with Thunderbird and one mph under the best time, recorded by the Grand Prix.

The Gran Sport package was still on the option list. So was air-conditioning, which was reduced to $421, and found on 36,251, or 84.7% of this year's Rivieras. It surpassed power windows in popularity, because 81.8% had the electric lifters—34,993 to be precise. The installation of disc brakes more than doubled, but the number was very small—just 2,905, which was 6%. The biggest increase for options was the vinyl roof, up seven times the number the year before. There were 21,773 with this option, which was just over half the year's model run.

Revised front-end styling for 1968 gave the Riviera a new and distinctive look, but there was not much mechanical change. The same 430 cubic inch motor with a single four-barrel carburetor was continued. Its developed horsepower remained at 360 could move about without embarrassing its driver. Tom McCahill did the 0 to 60 run in 8.1 seconds and found the top speed to be 125 plus. "World Car Catalog" said 132.

The Gran Sport option—mainly a high-performance suspension package—was still available at $132, and highly rated by the auto press. McCahill, referring to its handling, claimed his Riviera GS test car was "just about the best of any of the 1968 cars we have tested."

Superficial styling changes were applied to the 1969 Riviera. The headlights were still hidden, but it was the last year for that feature, which was losing popularity. Riviera continued offering a single body type, the two-door hardtop Sport Coupe. The $132 Gran Sport option, with its superior suspension was still offered.

The engine situation was virtually unchanged. There was a choice of one—the 430 cubic inch 360 hp V-8 with one four-barrel carburetor. It developed a hefty 475 ft-lbs of torque, which was among the most potent available at the time.

"Motor Trend" tested the Riviera and got a 9.2 second time in their 0 to 60 acceleration. For the standing-start quarter-mile, Riviera took 16.1 seconds, reaching 87.5 mph. "World Cars Catalog" still maintained that the Riviera's top speed was 132 mph.

A new grille was featured on the 1970 Riviera. Another change in the frontal appearance was the return to exposed headlights. But these differences were mainly superficial. The basic car remained much the same as before. Wheelbase was still 119 inches and overall length was also unchanged at 216 inches. Only 17 lbs was added to the Riviera's weight, now 4,199 lbs.

A new engine was featured, or perhaps it is more accurate to say the former engine was enlarged with 1/8 inch greater bore. It had a displacement of 455 cubic inches and developed 370 hp. That was the largest and most powerful engine used in a Riviera

or any other production Buick. It was rated at 10 hp more than the Stage I version for the 1970 mid-size Gran Sport. There were no engine options for Riviera.

This engine put some extra pep into Riviera's performance as the tests proved. Just 7.9 seconds was all the time Tom McCahill needed to go from 0 to 60. Maximum speed was still in the 125-plus mph area, he reported.

However, the high-performance era was passing. Riviera production of 37,336 was nearly a 30% tumble from the 1969 peak. A $153 price increase was added, making the list price $4,854. The Gran Sport suspension and appearance option was a bargain at $132—the price it had been for several years.

An all-new body made the 1971 Riviera look totally different. It had a fastback shape that ended in a boat-tail. It rode on a new chassis with a 122 inch wheelbase. Overall length was now 218 inches, a growth of 10 inches since the Riviera first appeared. The new body added 109 lbs so the total weight was 4,325.

The 455 cubic inch engine still powered the new Riviera. However, it was considerably altered to meet government emissions standards. For one thing, compression was reduced from 10:1 to a mild 8.5:1. In standard form, the end result was only 315 developed hp. There was a 330 hp option. It was added to the Gran Sport package, which continued to include heavy-duty suspension and Positraction differential. Its price was $200 and was an excellent value for all it had to offer.

Performance was affected by the heavier body and pollution prevention altered engines. The ubiquitous Tom McCahill put the 1971 Riviera through its paces, getting a 0 to 60 time of 8.1 seconds and a top speed of 120 mph. Not quite as good as before.

The Riviera's performance on ice or other slippery surfaces was enhanced by the MaxTrac. It was a computer-controlled device designed to eliminate skidding by breaking the engine ignition circuit. This device was initially a Riviera option before it was made available on other Buick models. Then it was quietly removed from the option list after the 1972 model year because it counteracted the more stringent emission control standards required for 1973 model cars.

The vinyl roof option was not quite as common on the 1971 Rivieras, perhaps because of the new body shape. There were 25,405 that had it. Still that was 75.1%.

A sizeable $399 increase put the Riviera's price at $5,253. The higher price and controversial styling probably accounted for the drop in production to 33,810. That was the fewest Rivieras built in any model year to date. It had fallen to being the fourth most popular Buick model.

For 1972, there was no great change to the Riviera because of the new body of the year before. The engine situation, however, was affected by increasingly stringent government requirements to reduce pollution. Due to the power-robbing side-effects of the anti-pollution equipment placed on the engine, only net horsepower ratings were published —not the gross figures—which were becoming preposterously low.

The only engine for the 1972 Riviera was the 455 cubic inch V-8. Its net horsepower rating was a disappointing 250. There were no alternatives, except the Gran Sport package included dual exhausts which raised the output a little but only to 260 net hp. The GS performance option was still $200 extra.

Naturally, performance fell below its earlier lofty peaks. "World Cars" (formerly "World Car Catalog") estimated Riviera's top speed to be 111 mph and, with the dual exhausts, 112 mph.

To encourage sales, the Riviera's price was reduced just over $100 to $5,149. That helped keep production just about the same as in 1971. It was 33,728, down 82 cars.

The third and last year for the fastback Riviera, 1973, saw only detail appearance differences. Beneath the hood, there were no great changes. The standard engine continued to be the 455 cubic inch motor that produced 250 net hp.

The only engine option was the dual exhaust version of the same motor, still rated at 260 hp. Beginning with the 1973 models, this option was given the Stage I name and cost $139 extra. The Gran Sport package was now separate from the engine option, as it had been prior to the 1972 models. It could be ordered with or without the Stage I engine. At $181, this suspension package now included steel-belted radial tires—the first for Riviera.

Another 143 lbs was gained from the year before. Some of the increase was attributable to the energy absorbing bumpers required by the Federal government. Yet, this 4,486 lb Riviera somehow managed to reach 112 mph maximum speed, or 113 with the dual exhaust option according to "World Cars."

Although the Riviera's popularity was still sagging at this time (sales for the calendar year were down nearly 18%), production of the 1973 model was increased a few hundred units to 34,080.

Riviera finally rid itself of the fastback styling for 1974, when a notchback coupe succeeded it. A remarkable job of reworking the former body was done. It was not a new body, but certainly looked like it was. Unfortunately, it lacked the distinction from other Buicks which had been characteristic of all the personal luxury Rivieras heretofore.

With the passing of the fastback styling, a Riviera tradition was ended. Until the 1974 model appeared, every one of the personal luxury Rivieras had been a hardtop. Even though Buick called the 1974 Riviera a Hardtop Coupe, it had center posts.

The big 455 cubic inch engine remained, but its output suffered from more emission control gadgets that had to be added. Consequently, it could only develop 230 hp in its basic version. The Stage I version was rated at 245 hp. Still offered was the GS handling package for $186 extra. It could be ordered with either engine.

Despite an 85 lb weight increase, maximum speed was raised in the 1974 models. "World Cars"

listed the Riviera's top speed at 127 mph with the standard engine and 130 with the Stage I option. Even if that was too optimistic, the Riviera undoubtedly could move briskly and, with the GS option, nimbly.

A $284 price hike greeted 1974 Riviera buyers. They were not forming long lines to sign purchase orders for this $5,505 car. Fuel economy was foremost in people's minds in 1974 and the Riviera was not outstanding in this regard. Ten mpg was normal for Riviera at this time so it was no wonder that production set a new low record. Only 20,129 were made—about half the number of its first year.

The notchback Riviera appeared again for 1975, but without much change in appearance. Changes were made to the engine, to keep up with annually increased anti-pollution standards set by the Federal government. Compression was lowered to 7.9:1, with a corresponding reduction in output to a meager 205 hp. Riviera, along with most other General Motors cars of 1975, was equipped with a catalytic converter in the exhaust system. Without it, further engine power would have been sapped in the anti-pollution drive. Unfortunately, there were no engine options for the 1975 Riviera.

There was a slight weight reduction. It was only 33 lbs, but a reduction of any size was better than an all-too-common increase. The car testers were not bothering with Riviera at this time, so 0 to 60 and standing-start quarter mile acceleration tests are practically impossible to find. "World Cars" continued its top speed estimates, listing the 1975 Riviera at 124 mph. Perhaps the car testers were overlooking something exciting.

This was the Riviera's darkest hour in terms of production. It was at its lowest point in all its years as a personal luxury car. Just 17,306 were built during the 1975 model year. Because it was Riviera's smallest production run, it has the distinction of being Riviera's rarest model. During the calendar

1974 Riviera

year, a scant 14,094 Rivieras were sold.

The GS suspension package was reduced to just $73. It probably did not include the steel-belted radial tires, which were now standard.

There was not much change in the 1976 Riviera, yet there were numerous hidden differences. Styling continued basically the same as before. Engine-wise, there was still the 455 cubic inch V-8. For the first time in five years, there was no reduction in the

horsepower rating. Output remained at 205. Like the year prior, there were no engine options.

Conspicuously absent from the option list was the GS high-performance handling package. It had been available on the Riviera beginning with the 1965 models and was a great favorite with the performance-minded buyers ever since. If it had not been for the GS option, Buick could only have sold a fraction of the high-performance cars they did.

1975 Riviera

In Review:
1985 High Performance Buicks.

By Paul North

Buick has been doing pretty well for itself during the past few years, managing to close in on Oldsmobile, the nation's third-best-selling car. In the process, Buick executives (those who can remember back that far) have been given to memories of the glory years of the 1950s, a time when Buick reigned supreme in the medium-priced field, second only to Ford and Chevy. Cadillacs were quite scarce back then, and had been even more so before the war. The Buick was considered the car of choice by many professional people who thought Cadillac ownership too extravagant, or pushy, or whatever. Needless to say, that was long before Cadillac hit 300,000 units a year in production and started building silly non-entities on the order of the Cimarron. Much has changed in the last thirty years!

Buick's recent success has been for much the same reasons as that of sister division, Oldsmobile: it has found a magic formula for the manufacture of the sort of family transportation middle class America has lately wanted to buy. While this has been good for the coffers in Flint, and has hardly hurt the careers of those involved, it hasn't done much for the spirit—especially unfortunate for a division that uses as its logo the American bald eagle matched with phrases such as "free spirited."

Fortunately, in the deep recesses of Buick City lurk a few dedicated souls who have labored feverishly to add some credibility to the advertising hype. Their creations have gone under the umbrella designation, "T-Type." There is, in fact, a T-Type of almost everything Buick builds, leading one to wonder if perhaps they haven't gone just a little bit overboard. There are T-Type C-cars, A-cars, J-cars, G-cars and E-cars. (The T-Type X-car was, mercifully,

1985 Regal T-Type Coupe

1985 Regal Grand National Coupe

deleted from the lineup for 1985.) If Buick built trucks, there would probably be 80,000 lb. GVW, sleeper cab, eighteen-wheeler T-Types rumbling across the prairie. (A provacative idea . . . wonder if the fellas at Peterbilt have thought of it?) Overall, Pontiac Motor Division probably has the better approach in limiting its "STE" designation to one model—and then making that one model really count. Still, you can't fault Buick for trying—and in at least one or two cases they have really come up with the goods.

The best of the bunch is probably the G-car: the Regal T-Type and its kissin' cousin, the Regal Grand National. These near-twins are not only near the top of the T-Type heap, they are just about the best G-cars being made by GM in 1985, meaning mostly the Monte Carlo SS, although Pontiac (Grand Prix) and Olds (Cutlass) build G-cars, too. The Monte Carlo SS is a nice try, but it doesn't have the finesse or attention to detail of the Regals. The Regals are faster off the line, they drive better and look a lot meaner, to boot.

The first thing you notice about the Regal T-Type and Grand National is their blacked-out trim. And, when we say "blacked-out," we mean it. They look at first glance as if the trim was left off by mistake, but

it is a look to which you soon become accustomed. Nothing on the road looks quite like it. Just about the only external brightwork of note are the handsome aluminum wheels, and even they are relatively understated by contemporary standards.

The interior is very nicely turned out, as well. The standard seats are fine and the instrumentation is complete and readable. Which brings us to an ugly little matter: Whatever you do, avoid the optional Lear Siegler bucket seats. These are supposed to be substitute Recaros, but they mostly are a pain in the backside. I first spent time with them when I tested a 1984 Century T-Type. For many hundreds of good, negotiable U.S. greenbacks, I was stuck with a pair of the most uncomfortable seats ever put in an automobile. The seats in my grandmother's 1949 Studebaker were better. Detroit often falls short of the mark, but these Lear Sieglers are genuinely disappointing. Pontiac and Chevy have pretty much stopped promoting them (though they remain lurking on the options list for some models). The 1985 versions seem to be better, but this is still one case where you don't get what you pay for.

Underneath, the Regal T-Type and Grand National are powered by Buick's own 3.8 liter V-6.

1985 BUICK REGAL T TYPE

PERFORMANCE

ACCELERATION

Time to distance, sec:
- 0-100 ft 4.1
- 0-500 ft 9.3
- 0-1320 ft (¼ mi) 16.1

Speed at end of ¼ mi .. 84 mph

Time to speed, sec:
- 0-30 .... 3.3
- 0-50 .... 6.2
- 0-60 .... 8.3

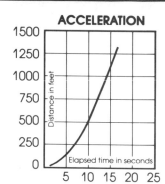

ACCELERATION

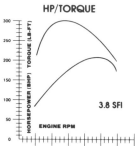

HP/TORQUE

3.8 SFI

HANDLING*

Max lateral
  accel, g .... .84

Roll gain .... 4.54 degrees
per g

Steering sensitivity ... 1.19g
per 100 degrees of
steering wheel angle

*One car sample

POWERTRAIN

ENGINE 3.8 Litre SFI Turbo V-6

Type .... Buick-Bosch sequential port fuel injected with electronic mass air flow system 90° V6 arrangement, computer controlled coil ignition and mass air flow sensor - designed underhood appearance.

Valve Arrangement .... Overhead Valve
Bore & Stroke (In.) 3.8x3.4
Displacement (cu.in.) 3.8L (231)
Cylinder Head &
  Block Material .... Cast Iron
Compression Ratio 8.0:1
Net/Installed Horsepower &
  Engine RPM .... 200 @ 4000
Net/Installed Torque (lb-ft)
  & Engine RPM .... 300 @ 2400
Recommended Fuel ...... No-lead Premium
Fuel System Type .... Port Fuel Inj.
EPA Fuel Estimates
(Adjusted):
  -City 17
  -Hwy 24

DRIVETRAIN

Transmission .... 4-spd automatic with Torque Conv. clutch
  Selector Pattern   PRN Ⓓ D21
Gear Ratio
  First 2.74
  Second 1.57
  Third 1.00
  Fourth .... .67
  Reverse (R) 2.07
Max Ratio at Stall (torque converter) .. 1.85
Cooling .... Water
Total Oil Capacity 22
  Drain & Refill (pts) 10
Final Drive Ratio 3.42

DIMENSIONS

EXTERIOR	COUPE
Length	200.6
Width	71.6
Height	54.6
Wheelbase	108.1
Front Tread	58.5
Rear Tread	57.7
INTERIOR (Front)	
Leg Room	42.8
Head Room	37.9
Shoulder Room	56.9
Hip Room	51.7
(Rear)	
Leg Room	36.4
Head Room	38.1
Shoulder Room	56.1
Hip Room	54.9
TRUNK	
Luggage Capacity (ft³)	16.2
FUEL TANK	
Refill (Capacity Gals)	18.1
WEIGHT	
Est. Base Curb (lbs)	3256

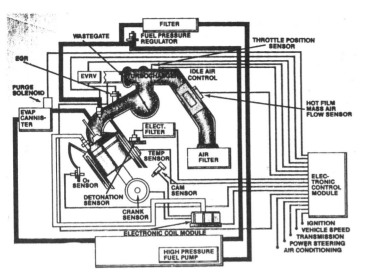

1985 3.8 SFI Turbo

This engine is standard in the ordinary Regal, but for the hot coupes, Buick turbocharges them and, for good measure, equips them with Sequential Port Fuel Injection. What that means is "very fast" in Buickese. SFI offers more precise fuel control than the Multi-Port fuel injection used on the Skyhawk Turbo, Skylark, Century and Electra. The system uses simultaneous double-fire injection: all six injectors are activated once during each engine revolution. In this way, two injections of fuel at the intake port are mixed with incoming air to produce the charge for each combustion cycle. The metered fuel is timed and injected into the individual ports immediately prior to the opening of the intake valve. Information to determine the precise timing and amount of fuel is provided by electronic sensors on the camshaft and crankshaft.

The Regal T-Type and Grand National are superlative automobiles. Buick has done a tremendous job with them. It is too bad that more enthusiasts haven't gotten into the habit of looking to Buick for high peformance hardware. Perhaps the word about this these machines will get out and begin to change that.

The new C-car Electra also has a T-Type. The Electra version has received quite a bit of publicity in the enthusiast press in recent months, often being compared (favorably) to the Audi 5000. The comparisons are surely apt in one regard: both cars are enormous by modern standards and hardly suited to more than gentlemanly touring. Still, the Electra is beautifully trimmed (far more so than the rather utilitarian Audi) and drives well within the obvious limitations imposed by its size. It may well be the best car in its league.

Buick has made another major effort with the A-car Century T-Type. In this case, the result is far over-shadowed by the superb Pontiac 6000 STE. The difference between the two cars is one of detail. The Pontiac has finesse in every little bit and piece important to a serious driving machine. The Buick, on the other hand, needs work. The Century T-Type I tested came equipped with the horrendous (but thankfully optional) Lear Siegler seats—which resulted in a week spent continuously trying (without success) to find a halfway comfortable driving position. That hardly helped my appreciation of the car, but it showed a lack of development in many other areas from instrumentation to handling. The Century is not a BAD car. If there weren't a Pontiac STE, it might seem much better than it does. But there is an STE and that is the one to buy.

The other T-Types, in Skyhawk and Riviera form, are mostly color and trim options. The Riviera

1985 Electra T-Type

1985 Electra T-Type

is handsome and the Skyhawk is very fast with its turbo, but neither of them rates as true drivers cars.

The final bit of news for 1985, is the Buick Somerset Regal. This is Buick's version of the N-car, also known as the Pontiac Grand Am and the Olds Calais. The Pontiac edition is the real drivers' car of the bunch (as far as it goes). The Olds is plain vanilla. The Buick, on the other hand, was designed to be a little Electra (and not even an Electra T-Type). It is a miniature luxo-barge, which is fine if that is what you want, but hardly qualifies it as enthusiast transportation.

In sum, then, Buick is in there trying, producing several serious enthusiast machines that rate the attention of any buff. The Regal T-Type and Grand National are at the top of the list, followed by the Electra T-Type, for those looking for a sporting luxo-cruiser, and the Century T-Type for those wanting a solid mid-size Buick. The trend is clearly toward performance in Buick City and Buick buffs are right to anticipate good things in years to come.

DIMENSIONS

EXTERIOR	COUPE	SEDAN
Length	196.2(4984)	196.2(4964)
Width	72.1(1832)	72.1(1832)
Height	55.0(1397)	55.0(1397)
Wheelbase	110.8(2815)	110.8(2815)
Front Tread	60.3(1532)	60.3(1532)
Rear Tread	59.7(1518)	59.7(1518)
INTERIOR (Front)		
Leg Room	42.4(1078)	42.4(1078)
Head Room	39.2(998)	39.2(998)
Shoulder Room	58.9(1496)	58.9(1496)
Hip Room	55.5(1409)	55.5(1409)
(Rear)		
Leg Room	40.8(1036)	40.8(1036)
Head Room	38.1(969)	38.1(969)
Shoulder Room	57.6(1464)	58.8(1494)
Hip Room	54.0(1372)	54.8(1393)
TRUNK		
Luggage Capacity	15.7(444)	15.7(444)
FUEL TANK		
Gal (litres)	18.0(68.2)	18.0(68.2)
WEIGHT		
(Est. Base Curb)	3216(1459)	3261(1459)

PERFORMANCE

ACCELERATION

Time to distance, sec:
- 0-100 ft 4.1
- 0-500 ft 10.4
- 0-1320 ft (¼ mi) 19.2

Speed at end of ¼ mi ... 74 mph

Time to speed, sec:
- 0-30 .... 4.1
- 0-50 .... 9.1
- 0-60 .... 12.6

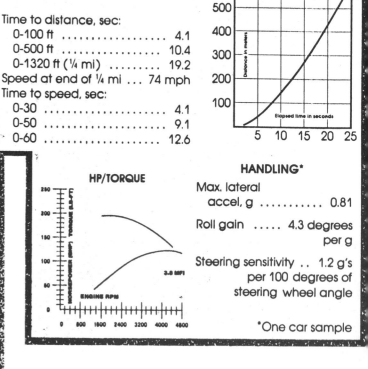

HANDLING*

Max. lateral
accel, g 0.81

Roll gain ..... 4.3 degrees
per g

Steering sensitivity .. 1.2 g's
per 100 degrees of
steering wheel angle

*One car sample

PERFORMANCE PERSPECTIVE

1985 Skyhawk T-Type Coupe

1985 Skyhawk Custom Coupe

1985 RIVIERA T TYPE COUPE

PERFORMANCE

ACCELERATION

Time to distance, sec:
- 0-100 ft 4.7
- 0-500 ft 10.4
- 0-1320 ft (¼ mi) 18.8

Speed at end of ¼ mi . . . . 79 mph

Time to speed, sec:
- 0-30 . . . . 4.2
- 0-50 . . . . 8.3
- 0-60 . . . . 11.1

ACCELERATION

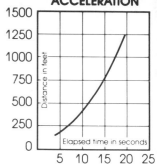

HP/TORQUE

HANDLING*

Max lateral
   accel, g 75
Roll gain . . . . 7.96 degrees
   per g.
Steering sensitivity . . . .93 g.
   per 100 degrees of
   steering wheel angle

*One car sample

POWERTRAIN

ENGINE 3.8 Litre SFI Turbo V-6

Type . . . . Buick-Bosch sequential port fuel injected with electronic mass air flow system 90° V6 arrangement, computer controlled coil ignition and mass air flow sensor - designed underhood appearance

Valve Arrangement . . . . Overhead Valve
Bore & Stroke (In.) . . . . 3.8 x 3.4
Displacement (cu.in) 3.8L (231)
Cylinder Head &
   Block Material . . . . Cast Iron
Compression Ratio 8.0:1
Net/Installed Horsepower &
   Engine RPM . . . . 190 @ 4000
Net/Installed Torque (lb-ft)
   & Engine RPM . . . . 300 @ 2400
Recommended Fuel . . . . . . No-lead Premium
Fuel System Type . . . . Port Fuel Injection
EPA Fuel Estimates
(Adjusted):
   -City 16
   -Hwy 24

DRIVETRAIN

Transmission
   Type . . . . 4 spd automatic with torque Conv. clutch
Selector Pattern . . . . PRN Ⓓ D21
Gear Ratio
   First 2.74
   Second 1.57
   Third 1.00
   Fourth 0.67
   Reverse (R) 2.07
Max Ratio at Stall 2.15
   (torque converter)
Cooling . . . . Water
Total Oil Capacity . . . . 5 Liter
   Drain & Refill (pts) . . . . . . 10.5 pts
Final Drive Ratio: 3.15

DIMENSIONS

EXTERIOR	COUPE
Length	206.6
Width	70.7
Height	54.3
Wheelbase	114.0
Front Tread	59.3
Rear Tread	60.0
INTERIOR (Front)	
Leg Room	42.8
Head Room	37.9
Shoulder Room	55.8
Hip Room	53.7
(Rear)	
Leg Room	39.2
Head Room	37.9
Shoulder Room	55.9
Hip Room	49.0
TRUNK	
Luggage Capacity (ft³)	15.8
FUEL TANK	
Refill (Capacity Gals)	21.1
WEIGHT	
Est. Base Curb (lbs)	3564

1985 Riviera T-Type Coupe

1985 Somerset Regal Limited Coupe

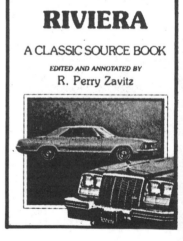
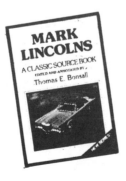